Student workbook for

Understanding Israel

MORRIS J. SUGARMAN

Behrman House, Inc. / Publishers / New York

Acknowledgments

I wish to say thank you to several people for the invaluable help that they have given me in the preparation of this workbook: Mrs. Gerry Gould, managing editor of Behrman House, who supervised its production, with her usual blending of warmth, involvement, and keen judgment; Karen Rossel, whose reading of the original manuscript resulted in so many improvements; Marilyn Wilson, who typed the manuscript with her characteristic patience and good humor; and Jacalyn O'Shaughnessy, who cut-and-pasted so conscientiously and imaginatively.

And I particularly thank Seymour Rossel, executive editor of Behrman House, who worked with me throughout this entire project. His contributions—from original conception to final execution—have been manifold and indispensable.

Book design — Marvin Friedman

© Copyright 1977 by BEHRMAN HOUSE, INC.

Published by BEHRMAN HOUSE, INC.

1261 Broadway, New York, New York 10001

ISBN: 0-87441-267-6

This asterisk * appears before exercises for which answers can be found in the Answer Key, pages 209-19.

PHOTOGRAPHS COURTESY OF Israel Ministry of Tourism, pages 1, 97, 159, and the Consulate General of Israel, page 129.

To Rivkah, and to the memory of Mechtzi,
who helped me understand — and love — Israel.

Unit One
Toward an Understanding

Chapter One

Israel, the Unique State

PERSONAL IMPRESSIONS OF ISRAEL

1. Underline five words from the following list that come closest to expressing your impressions of Israel today.

    poor   fearful   isolated   industrious   courageous

    suspicious   creative   different   Jewish   special

    endangered   scapegoat   melting pot   miracle

    pioneering nation

2. Using the five words that you have chosen, insert one word into each sentence below (after "is"). Then complete each sentence with a brief explanation of the particular description. For example: "Israel is an underdog (a word not included in the list above) because its army is greatly outnumbered by the armies of the surrounding Arab nations."

    a. Israel is _____ because _____

    _____

    _____

    _____

    b. Israel is _____ because _____

    _____

    _____

    _____

    c. Israel is _____ because _____

    _____

    _____

    _____

d. Israel is _____ because _____

_____

_____

e. Israel is _____ because _____

_____

_____

GENERAL KNOWLEDGE*

How would you rate your general knowledge of Israel? The following questions should give you some indication of where you stand at this point. The answers can be found on page 209.

1. When was Israel formally declared a sovereign state? (Give the year and, if possible, the month and day.) _____

2. Who was Israel's first prime minister? _____

3. Name any two other Israeli prime ministers. _____

_____

4. Who was Israel's first president? _____

_____

5. Who is called "the father of modern Zionism"? _____

6. How many major wars has Israel fought with its Arab neighbors since becoming a sovereign state?_____

7. Israelis have given each of these wars a name. What are they?

_____

_____

_____

8. In which one of the following years did Israel not fight a major war with the Arabs? (Circle one.)

   (a) 1967   (b) 1948   (c) 1961   (d) 1973   (e) 1956

9. Which of the following states does not share a border with Israel? (Circle one.)

   (a) Jordan   (b) Syria   (c) Iraq   (d) Lebanon

4

10. What is the Hebrew word meaning "pioneer" that has been used to describe the early Zionist settlers? _____

11. One of the most important contributions of the early pioneers was the creation of a collective community dedicated to a life of labor on the land and to the principle of equality. What is the community called?

_____

12. Jewish immigration to Israel is called aliyah. Which of the following words is its English translation? (Circle one.)

    (a) redemption   (b) ascent   (c) freedom   (d) immigration

    (e) fulfillment

13. Match the Israeli cities in the left column with the description in the right column that fits them most accurately.

    a. Haifa   _____ The city of David

    b. Tel Aviv   _____ The gateway to the Negev

    c. Jerusalem   _____ Israel's southernmost port

    d. Beersheba   _____ Located on Mount Carmel

    e. Eilat   _____ Israel's largest city

14. Which of the following cities is not bordered by the sea? (Circle one.)

    (a) Tel Aviv   (b) Jerusalem   (c) Haifa   (d) Jaffa

    (e) Ashkelon

15. Which figure most closely approximates the population of Israel today? (Circle one.)

    (a) 5 million   (b) 1.5 million   (c) 3 million   (d) 4.5 million

    (e) 7 million

16. True or false? (Check *T* if true, *F* if false.) The Zionist settlers who arrived in Palestine in the early 1880's were the first Jews to set foot in that land since the destruction of the Second Temple, nearly 2000 years ago. T [ ]   F [ ]

ISRAEL AND THE JEWISH PEOPLE

Imagine that you have a pen pal whose grandparents immigrated to this country from Italy. He or she wants to know something about the special relationship that exists between the Jewish people and Israel, and in what sense this relationship differs from the ties between Italian-Americans (or any other ethnic group) and their country of origin.

1. How would you explain this special relationship in two or three sentences?

2. Can you point out at least two differences in attitudes, education, or organizational activity between the Jewish people and other ethnic groups in this country, in terms of their relationships to their respective homelands?

3. Is Israel a part of your life in any way? If so, what effect has it had upon you?

ISRAEL'S UNIQUENESS

The Four Questions posed at the beginning of the Passover Seder can be used to help focus upon ways in which Israel is unique, set apart from other peoples and nations. Why is the State of Israel different from all other states? Fill in the following blank spaces with what you believe to be appropriate answers:

1. Whereas other states were created by people who have always lived

   together in one place, Israel _____

   _____

2. Whereas most states are intimately related to other states in terms of either language, culture, or religion, Israel _____

_____

3. Whereas all states define their primary involvement and commitment within their national borders, Israel _____

_____

4. Whereas all states take their existence and survival for granted, Israel

_____

_____

WORD SCRAMBLE*

Unscramble the following words, each of which is closely connected in some way with modern Israel. Then unscramble the seven letters that are within the circles to make a word which played a crucial role in the creation of the Jewish state.

1. vegne

2. zelhr

3. fihaa

4. wejhis

5. rohah

6. surelejam

Chapter Two

View from the Grandstand

A SEARCH FOR UNDERSTANDING *

1. Which of the following adjectives does not apply to the individuals discussed in this chapter, and why?

    (a) Committed   (b) Passionate   (c) Quarrelsome

    (d) Nonpolitical   (e) Idealistic

    _____

    _____

2. Can you cite at least two reasons why the vatikim embraced Zionism and immigrated to Israel?

    (a) _____

    (b) _____

3. True or false? At the time of the 1968 Independence Day Parade, Zalman Shazar was the most politically powerful official in Israel.
    T [ ]   F [ ]

4. Match the individual in the left column with the description in the right column that fits most accurately.

    a. Zalmar Shazar   _____ A cause of parental worry

    b. Golda Meir   _____ A desert dweller

    c. Moshe Dayan   _____ A marathon public speaker

    d. Levi Eshkol   _____ A pioneer from the United
                                    States

    e. Rachel Yanait Ben-Zvi _____ A supporter of compromise
                                    and cooperation

    f. David Ben-Gurion   _____ A native of Kibbutz
                                    Degania

5. Aside from the fact that he was much younger than any of the other leaders discussed in the chapter, Moshe Dayan is described as being dif-

8

ferent, set apart from everyone else. Can you point out at least three differences between Dayan and his elders?

_____

_____

_____

6. Which of the following personalities did not serve as a public official after Israel became a sovereign state? (Circle one.)

   (a) Levi Eshkol   (b) Rachel Yanait Ben-Zvi   (c) Moshe Dayan

   (d) David Ben-Gurion   (e) Golda Meir

7. For all of their differences, the vatikim were strikingly similar to one another in terms of background, outlook, and values. In two or three sentences, sum up what you think are the most important of their common characteristics.

   _____

   _____

   _____

   _____

IDENTIFICATION*

1. The title of the Russian ruler at the time that David Ben-Gurion and Levi Eshkol set out for Palestine   _____

2. A native-born Israeli   _____

3. Israel's first kibbutz   _____

4. The name of the Negev kibbutz in which Ben-Gurion lived in semi-retirement   _____

5. The English word used to describe Jewish life outside of the Jewish homeland   _____

6. A violent assault upon the Jewish community by neighboring non-Jews   _____

7. The land offered to Theodor

Herzl (and rejected by the
Russian Zionists) as a Jewish
homeland by the British
government   _____

THE PIONEER'S JEWISH BACKGROUND

Whatever their personal qualities, the vatikim shared an intense and encompassing Jewish background. What were the elements that defined the
Jewish experience in Eastern Europe at the turn of the century? In the
categories below, write one or two sentences that point up the specifically
Jewish nature of the vatikim's early lives. (Appearance : most Jewish men
in Eastern Europe grew beards and payot — earlocks or sideburns.)

1. Language _____

    _____

    _____

2. Education _____

    _____

    _____

3. Economic conditions _____

    _____

    _____

4. Physical security_____

    _____

    _____

5. Relationship with non-Jews _____

    _____

    _____

    _____

6. Political situation (legal position, treatment by government officials,

    etc.)_____

    _____

    _____

7. Anti-Semitism _____

_____

_____

AN INTENSIVE JEWISH LIFE

The vatikim came from one kind of intensive Jewish environment and hoped to create a Jewish life at least as intensive (though dramatically different) in Eretz Israel. How would you define an intensive Jewish life? What are its essential ingredients, in your opinion?

ISSUES IN DEPTH

Support each of the general statements below with a specific quotation (a sentence or two at most) from the text.

1. David Ben-Gurion was an optimist and a visionary.

_____

_____

_____

2. Zalman Shazar was a man of many talents.

_____

_____

_____

3. Levi Eshkol believed that the differences between rival factions could be discussed and ultimately worked out.

_____

_____

4. Golda Meir did not foresee the disappearance of anti-Semitism in the near future.

_____

_____

_____

5. Rachel Yanait Ben-Zvi was an outspoken idealist with the courage of her convictions.

_____

_____

_____

WHO AM I? *

1. I have been around since the earliest days of Zionist settlement. My name expresses the passionate hopes shared by the pioneers.

2. I am a member of the Russian group most often associated with violent attacks upon Jewish communities.

3. I am the political philosophy that was embraced by Russian revolutionaries—non-Jews and Jews—at the turn of the century.

4. I have been described as filthy and depressing, but I can boast of several distinctions. For example, I was the first place in which the Zionist pioneers set foot when they arrived in Eretz Israel.

5. I am a declaration made at the end of Yom Kippur and I express a longing deeply rooted in the consciousness of the Jewish people during the 2000 years that they have been in exile.

FOR AND AGAINST ALIYAH

Imagine a going-away party for a group of young pioneers about to leave for Palestine. Their families and neighbors admire their courage, but are dismayed at the prospect of this "adventure to nowhere." In the course of discussion, the following arguments are made against going to Palestine. Fill in what you believe might have been the pioneers' responses.

1. Palestine is a land that has been neglected for centuries. It reeks of decay and disease.

    _____

    _____

    _____

2. How will you make a living?

    _____

    _____

    _____

3. Think of the dangers that you will have to face—Arab marauders, unfriendly officials, and God knows what else.

    _____

    _____

    _____

4. What kind of Jews will you become? What sort of Jewish community do you hope to create in that wilderness?

    _____

    _____

    _____

Chapter Three

Zionism as a Revolution

COMPONENTS OF THE ZIONIST REVOLUTION

---

1. The term revolution has been overused and distorted in recent years. How would you define revolution? What are its key characteristics? What factors and forces are most likely to bring it about?

   _____

   _____

   _____

   _____

   _____

2. The chapter points out that the Zionist revolution "taught a persecuted people to help themselves." In what sense can Zionism be described as a formula for self-help?

   _____

   _____

   _____

3. List at least three specific changes in Jewish life that have come about because of the Zionist revolution.

   _____

   _____

   _____

   _____

4. One of the most significant outgrowths of the Zionist revolution has been the sabra, the Israeli born and raised in a Jewish state. How does the sabra differ from a Jew born and raised outside of Israel in the following spheres?

   a. Language _____

   _____

b. Education _____

_____

c. Responsibilities _____

_____

d. Political status _____

_____

e. Anti-Semitism (as expressed in attitudes and/or policies) _____

_____

f. Culture _____

_____

_____

g. Contact with world Jewry _____

_____

5. True or false? *

   a. The Zionist revolution has fulfilled all of its aims. T [   ] F [   ]

   b. Two of Zionism's most prominent achievements have been the revival of Hebrew as a living language, and the creation of the kibbutz. T [   ] F [   ]

   c. The Jewish people today have opportunities that were not available to them before the Zionist revolution. T [   ] F [   ]

   d. Jews were always well-treated in Muslim countries before the establishment of the state of Israel. T [   ] F [   ]

   e. The situation of the Arab refugees is partially a result of the actions and decisions of various Arab leaders. T [   ] F [   ]

6. How would you define the phrase "prisoners in spirit"?

_____

_____

_____

7. Can you point to modern examples of "prisoners in spirit" from your own knowledge and/or experience?

_____

_____

_____

WORD SCRAMBLE*

Unscramble the words in each of the following; and then rearrange them to express a fundamental aim of modern Zionism. (Example: akme a vilnig ot agew = make living to wage a = To make a living wage)

1. fo a now rou nald = _____

    _____ = _____

2. sejw a veahn orf = _____

    _____ = _____

3. rofm eitammissint demoref = _____

    _____ = _____

4. bewher levirav fo = _____

    _____ = _____

5. sujt a teosyci whesij = _____

    _____ = _____

CAUSES AND EFFECTS

The following elements are recognized as the causes of many revolutions. Define each of these in specifically Jewish terms. For example: Dissatisfaction with the status quo — The Jewish people bitterly complained about the inability or unwillingness of the government to protect them from physical violence.

1. The failure of a system or a society to meet the crucial needs of its members

    _____

    _____

    _____

2. A recognition of that failure by the people in question

    _____

    _____

    _____

3. General agreement as to the cause or causes of this failure

_____

_____

4. A leader or leaders able to inspire the people to embark upon a revolutionary course

_____

_____

_____

5. The means, in whatever form, of realizing revolutionary aims

_____

_____

_____

ZIONISM AS A REMEDY

One reason that the Zionist revolution came into being is because a significant number of Jews found their lives in the Diaspora difficult, dangerous, and often intolerable. They saw Zionism as a remedy, perhaps the only remedy, for their assorted problems. The statements below express some of the more serious Jewish complaints before the creation of the Jewish state. In the spaces following each statement, write a sentence or two describing the remedy provided by the Zionist revolution for that complaint. If the problem persists despite the existence of Israel, say so and explain why.

1. No matter where we live, or for how long, Jews are always strangers.

_____

_____

2. We are a minority at the mercy of the will and whim of the majority.

_____

_____

3. To some extent, the Jew must play the role of a chameleon, taking on the shape and coloring of the particular surroundings.

_____

_____

4. In the best of circumstances, we are persistently haunted by anti-Semitism. It may go into hiding for a time, but it is always there, ready to pounce; in that sense, we are permanently in danger.

_____

_____

5. Assimilation is a constant worry, maybe the biggest threat to Jewish survival in the long run.

_____

_____

6. Our biggest problem is Jewish illiteracy. Fewer and fewer people know their history or tradition. And before too long, not knowing can become not caring.

_____

_____

REFUTING DISTORTIONS

Two factors have endlessly aided anti-Semitism and anti-Zionism: misinformation and illogic. See if you can refute the following accusations either on the basis of what you know or with simple, straightforward logic.

1. Israel is solely responsible for the plight of the Arab refugees today.

_____

_____

_____

2. The Arabs living in Israel today are helpless, oppressed, and without hope.

_____

_____

_____

3. I know that Zionism is a form of racism because it has been condemned as such by the UN General Assembly in November 1975.

_____

_____

_____

PHOTO STUDY

Examine the photograph on page 22 of the text, and answer the following questions on the basis of its contents:

1. What differences can you point out between the Jews in this picture and the Jews of your community?

   _____

   _____

   _____

2. Why is their immigration referred to as a "shift of population"?

   _____

   _____

   _____

3. Why are they called refugees?

   _____

   _____

   _____

4. What do you think caused them to leave their lands of origin?

   _____

   _____

   _____

5. Draw up a checklist of "important things to be done" to absorb these immigrants into Israeli life socially, culturally, and economically.

   _____

   _____

   _____

   _____

6. Name at least two major problems that these immigrants are likely to face as they try to adapt to Israeli life.

   _____

   _____

   _____

Chapter Four

A Nation Comes of Age

A SEARCH FOR UNDERSTANDING*

1. Which of the following factors did not contribute in some way to the outbreak of the Six Day War? (Circle one.)

    a. Pre-war tensions between Israel and Syria

    b. Soviet ambitions in the Middle East

    c. Israel's desire for a united Jerusalem

    d. UN miscalculations and ineffectiveness

    e. Nasser's push for power in the Arab world

2. Which of the following developments cannot be considered a result, direct or indirect, of the Six Day War? (Circle one.)

    a. The War of Attrition

    b. More extensive contacts with Arabs outside of Israel

    c. The Arab Summit Conference of Khartoum

    d. A surge of Israeli optimism and confidence

    e. Improved prospects for Arab-Israeli peace

3. In a sentence or two, explain why the Palestinian refugees are sometimes called "the Jews of the Middle East."

    _____

    _____

    _____

4. In which of the following ways do Israelis differ from their Arab neighbors? (Circle one.)

    a. They speak a Semitic language

    b. They are beset by social and/or economic problems

    c. They are confronted by the constant possibility of war

    d. They are threatened with national destruction

    e. They belong to the United Nations

5. In what sense did its victory in the Six Day War mark Israel's coming-of-age, according to the text?

_____

_____

_____

_____

6. The Soviet Union's anti-Israel posture and its active, often aggressive, support of the Arab cause in the Middle East conflict since the mid-fifties has been widely acknowledged as a major contributing factor to the continuing state of hostility between Arabs and Israelis. Which of the following reasons is the least likely motive for Soviet maneuverings in the Middle East, and why?

   a. The Soviet Union's long-standing tradition of anti-Semitism

   b. The Soviet aim of acquiring power and influence in the Arab world

   c. The militarily strategic importance of the Middle East in terms of Soviet-American rivalry

   d. The Soviet desire to gain prestige with Third World nations

_____

_____

_____

7. Which of the following was not a factor in the long-standing Arab refusal to recognize Israel's right to exist, and why?

   a. Arab nationalism

   b. Arab territory captured by Israel during the Six Day War

   c. Inter-Arab rivalries

   d. The ambitions of certain Arab leaders

   e. The Arab belief that Israel should, can, and, one day, will be destroyed

_____

_____

_____

8. True or false? The Six Day War was a tragedy of errors. If the Arabs had only realized that there were no Israeli troops massed on the Syrian border, hostilities would have been avoided. T [ ] F [ ]

MAP STUDY *

The map below depicts Israel just before the outbreak of the Six Day War,
surrounded on its northern, southern, and eastern borders by Arab armies
poised for attack, and by the Mediterranean Sea to the west. On the basis of
what is shown and implied on this map, answer the following questions:

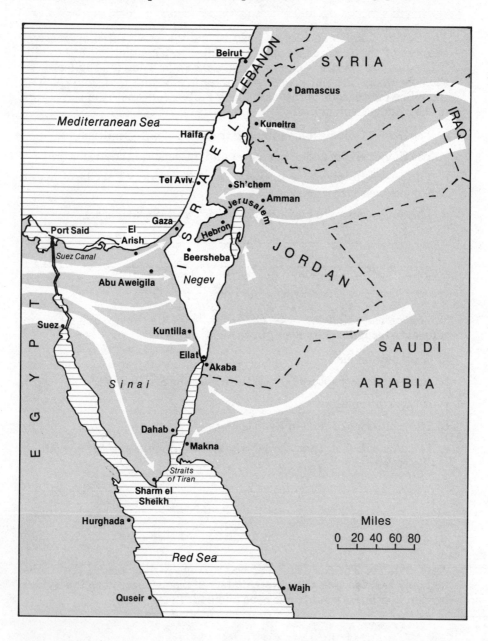

1. True or false? If the Israeli army were to be pushed back, forced to retreat, it would have nowhere to go. The battleground would become the cities, towns, and villages of the Jewish state itself. T [   ]   F [   ]

2. The army of which Arab state could, by a successful forward thrust, cut Israel into two? (Circle one.)

   a. Egypt   b. Syria   c. Iraq   d. Jordan   e. Lebanon

3. One of the most important fringe benefits of Israel's victory in the Six Day War has been the variety of advantages, military and otherwise, that it has gained by the capture of the Sinai Peninsula, the West Bank, and the Golan Heights. Match the following advantages with one of the three areas: Write S for Sinai, W for West Bank, and G for the Golan Heights.

   a. Straightened (and, therefore, far more defensible) borders [   ]

   b. Secure passage to the Red Sea [   ]

   c. Relief from artillery barrages in the Upper Galilee [   ]

   d. A united Jerusalem [   ]

   e. Long range military strategic depth [   ]

   f. An opportunity for contact with citizens from neighboring Arab countries [   ]

4. Identify the following:

   a. The Syrian town taken by the Israelis in their capture of the Golan Heights_____

   _____

   b. The port city sandwiched (before 1967) between two Arab states

   _____

   c. Two ancient Israelite cities located on the West Bank _____

   _____

   d. The area bordered by the Mediterranean Sea which contained many refugee camps, and served as a launching center for terrorist raids into Israel, before it was captured in 1967 _____

   _____

   e. The location at the tip of the Sinai Peninsula where an Israeli presence has helped save the Jewish state's right of free navigation through the Straits of Tiran and into the Red Sea _____

   _____

HISTORY'S HEADLINES *

A newspaper headline must sum up events, major and minor, in a few well-chosen words. On the basis of information contained in this chapter, to which Arab-Israeli war does each of the following headlines refer (the War of Attrition is included here, as is the Yom Kippur War)?

1. ISRAEL AND ALLIES REACH CANAL

2. SOVIETS AND AMERICANS CONDEMN ARAB ATTACK

3. MEN POUR OUT OF SYNAGOGUES TO JOIN ARMY UNITS

4. ISRAELIS DENY TROOP BUILD-UP

5. U.S. PRESSURES FRANCE AND ENGLAND TO WITHDRAW FROM EGYPT

6. ISRAELIS SHOCKED BY SURPRISE ATTACK

7. FRONTLINE SOLDIERS MARK FIRST ANNIVERSARY OF WAR, WONDER WHEN IT WILL END

8. ENVOY 'NYETS' INVITATION TO SEE FOR HIMSELF

9. SHIPMENT OF CZECH ARMS LIFTS ISRAELI SPIRITS

10. "WAITING WORSE THAN WAR ITSELF," DECLARE ISRAELIS

CREATING HEADLINES

This is a mirror image of the preceding activity, an exercise in creativity. In the previous section, you were asked to deduce a particular event from the content of the headline. The aim here is to compose a headline to fit the event. Remember, headlines are not only supposed to tell the news; they are supposed to help sell the news—make it dramatic and exciting. Afterward you might compare notes with your classmates to see what they have concocted, or have a contest for the most imaginative headline, or organize a headline quiz.

1. The 1967 Arab Summit Conference in Khartoum

    _____

2. The rejection by Arab leaders of UN testimony that there were no Israeli troop concentrations on the Syrian border

    _____

3. The removal of the United Nations Emergency Force as a buffer between Israel and Egypt

    _____

4. The Arab invasion of Israel directly after the creation of the Jewish state in 1948

    _____

5. The entry of Israeli soldiers into the refugee camps and their reactions to what they saw

    _____

ISSUES IN DEPTH

Support each of the general statements below with a specific quotation from the text (a sentence or two at most).

1. Israel, clearly the underdog in the Six Day War, achieved victory against all odds.

    _____

    _____

    _____

    _____

2. After the Six Day War, the Israelis were willing to take risks for peace.

_____

_____

_____

3. The Israelis, despite their victory, were troubled by the consequences of war.

_____

_____

_____

4. Even after its defeat, Egypt did not give up hope of using military means against Israel.

_____

_____

_____

5. Telling the truth (about the alleged massing of Israeli troops on the Syrian border) would not have prevented the Six Day War.

_____

_____

_____

6. In the months following the Six Day War, the Arab leaders were not interested in making a settlement with Israel.

_____

_____

_____

7. The Soviet Union bears a direct responsibility for the outbreak of the Six Day War.

_____

_____

_____

Unit Two
Zionism and the First Aliyah
1881 – 1905

Chapter Five

Eastern European Origins

MATCHING DESCRIPTIONS*

Match the terms in the left column with the descriptions in the right column. To add an extra element of challenge (or confusion) to this activity, there are six terms and only five matching descriptions. Identify the term that is not described below.

1. Pale of Settlement

    ____ The Jewish version of the European Enlightenment

2. Shtetl

    ____ A close-knit Jewish community, characterized by a sense of caring and responsibility

3. "Tradition on wheels"

    ____ The area in Eastern Europe where the overwhelming majority of Jews were required to live

4. Haskalah

    ____ The name describing the towns and villages in which most Russian Jews lived

5. Der goldene medine

    ____ Keeping laws, life-style, and values intact regardless of where they (the Jewish people) happened to live, or in what set of circumstances

6. Kehillah

The term with no matching description is

ISSUES IN DEPTH

Support each of the general statements below with a specific quotation from the text.

1. Open anti-Semitism could be found at the highest levels of government in Russia.

   _____

   _____

   _____

2. Russia in the late nineteenth century was ripe for revolution.

   _____

   _____

   _____

3. Hatred of the Jew was not confined to any one group; everyone indulged.

   _____

   _____

   _____

4. The Jews of Eastern Europe were prepared to preserve their identity at all costs.

   _____

   _____

   _____

5. Jewish history, tradition, hopes, and dreams all played an active role in the life of the shtetl.

   _____

   _____

   _____

6. The concept of community, expressed in terms of closeness and mutual responsibility, is an important value in Jewish tradition.

   _____

   _____

   _____

7. Most Eastern European Jews did not assimilate into the society and culture of the non-Jewish majority, but remained a people apart.

_____

_____

_____

8. Despite its problems, uncertainties, sufferings, and tragedies, modern Jewish history can be characterized as an extremely creative period.

_____

_____

_____

TRUE OR FALSE? *

1. At the turn of the century, there were nearly as many Jews in Russia as there are in Israel today. T [   ]   F [   ]

2. The majority of Russian Jews had roots in that country which went back at least 500 years. T [   ]   F [   ]

3. The anti-Semitic violence suffered by Russian Jews at the end of the nineteenth century was the product of both official policies and popular attitudes. T [   ]   F [   ]

4. One of the major problems confronting the communities in the Pale of Settlement was assimilation into Russian society, and an abandonment of Jewish life and tradition. T [   ]   F [   ]

5. Among other reasons, Jews in Russia were persecuted because they were an island of prosperity in a sea of poverty. Politically helpless, most Russian Jews were economically well-off. T [   ]   F [   ]

CREATIVE RESPONSES *

Let us further explore the phenomenon of Jewish creativity. The text points out, "The last two centuries included the following developments: the rise of the Hassidic movement; the *Haskalah* (the Jewish Enlightenment); the development of Yiddish literature; the rebirth of Hebrew as a living language and the beginnings of modern Hebrew literature; Reform Judaism; the Jewish *Bund* (Socialist) Movement; the establishment of a strong American Jewish community; modern Zionism; the kibbutz; and, finally, the creation of the State of Israel" (page 37). Each of these developments was clearly a response to a deep-seated yearning. Below are expressions of the kinds of needs and/or aspirations that have characterized Jewish life in recent times. Fill in the blank spaces with the creative response that was made to the particular yearning described.

1. Songs, poems, and stories in a language that expresses the heart and soul of the shtetl

   _____

2. To be a majority instead of a permanent minority, first-class citizens in a land of our own

   _____

3. To create a culture rooted in our ancient past

   _____

4. To live in a country that promises religious freedom instead of endless persecution, economic opportunity instead of unrelieved poverty

   _____

5. To fashion a community not only based upon *where* we are, but upon *who* we are, an expression of our deepest values

   _____

ADVANTAGES AND DISADVANTAGES

Many Jews who left their shtetls to begin a new life in the United States did so with mixed feelings. From a Jewish standpoint, each setting had advantages and disadvantages. Make a checklist of these advantages and disadvantages to gain a clearer idea of the factors and forces that came into play when Jews had to decide whether to remain in their places of origin or to leave.

1. The shtetl

   a. Advantages

   _____

   _____

   _____

   _____

   _____

b. Disadvantages

_____

_____

_____

_____

2. The United States

a. Advantages

_____

_____

_____

_____

b. Disadvantages

_____

_____

_____

_____

A PROFILE OF SHTETL LIFE

Life in the shtetl featured a variety of experiences, ranging from the beauty of a Sabbath celebration to the horror of a pogrom. What was it like to live in that time and place? We will never truly know, but we can imagine, and with the help of the text we should be able to come up with some interesting impressions.

In the space below, do a brief profile (in any manner or medium - a descriptive paragraph, a drawing, a poem, an anecdote, snatches of dialogue, etc.) of a particular shtetl experience. Possibilitites for such a profile include: a family gathered to greet the Sabbath; Yeshivah students arguing a point of holy Law; the weekly market day; a farewell party for friends immigrating to America; a band of neighboring peasants who drink too much and threaten to turn ugly; a Jewish wedding. Afterward, you might want to compare creative notes with your classmates to gain a broader view of the shtetl experience.

DEFINING JEWISH VALUES

In your own words, point out the Jewish values, attitudes, and character traits that are reflected in the following statements:

1. Eastern European Jews preferred banishment and death to conversion.

    _____

    _____

    _____

2. A brilliant Yeshivah student, as poor as he might be, enjoyed a high degree of status in the shtetl.

    _____

    _____

    _____

3. For all of the suffering that they endured in Eastern Europe, Jews who immigrated to America continued to refer to their native towns and villages as der "haim " (the home) .

_____

_____

_____

4. Though physically in the middle of Russia or Poland, in their hearts they were residents of an imaginary Jerusalem.

_____

_____

_____

5. The poorest Jew would be a prince in his home on Friday night, as his family sat around the table waiting for him to recite the blessing over wine that would begin the Sabbath celebration.

_____

_____

_____

Chapter Six

Three Avenues of Escape

A SEARCH FOR UNDERSTANDING *

---

1. Which of the following choices was *not* realistically open to Eastern European Jewry at the turn of the century? (Circle one.)

    a. Immigrating to America   b. Embracing Zionism
    c. Accepting the situation and making the best of it   d. Conversion
    e. Working within the system to bring about a change for the better
    f. Political radicalism

2. _____ is a Hebrew acronym for the Zionist group formed in the early 1880's. Its English translation is

   _____

3. True or false? Those who sought various avenues of escape were, in fact, a minute percentage of Eastern European Jewry. T [   ]   F [   ]

4. An Arab ambassador to the Soviet Union might, with some justice, level the following accusation at his Russian hosts: "It is your country that is responsible for the troubles we have today. If it weren't for you, there would be no Zionist movement, no Israel, and no large and influential Jewish community in the United States." Briefly explain what he is saying and why.

   _____

   _____

   _____

   _____

5. Which of the descriptions below cannot be applied to the Jewish Bund? (Circle one.)

    a. Yiddish speaking   b. In favor of political revolution   c. Had ties with non-Jewish political groups   d. Supported Jewish national revival   e. Involved with labor causes   f. Had nothing in common with the Zionist movement

6. Which of the descriptions below cannot be applied to the Russian Zionists? (Circle one.)

a. Believed in social revolution   b. Influenced by the radical ideas of the times   c. Foresaw a time when Jews would be free, fulfilled, and unafraid wherever they lived   d. Embraced Zionism partly because of lack of opportunities in Russia

A SCRAMBLED STORY*

Unscramble the words below. Then write them in the appropriate blank spaces to complete the paragraph that follows.

sopariad   _____

marpencene   _____

cesganip   _____

malohend   _____

saridilmac   _____

noissitz   _____

tidytine   _____

Russian Jews were assaulted on every side, and urgently looked for means

of _____ from their desperate situation. A majority of these Jews showed their willingness to try yet another (though more congenial)

_____ setting by immigrating to America. Others sincerely

believed _____ was the means of creating a better world, a world of international brotherhood, undivided by differences of race, religion, or national boundaries, and often showed a disturbing tendency to

negate their _____ in the name of a larger cause. The

_____ rejected both of these solutions in favor of a Jewish

_____, for they believed, among other things, in the

_____ of anti-Semitism.

INSIGHTS

1. In your own words, explain why the Zionists believed that:

   a. Anti-Semitism was an incurable disease.

   b. The Diaspora Jew would always be a stranger.

   c. The Jewish people needed a political homeland.

   d. This homeland should be the land of Israel.

2. What point was the Zionist student trying to make with the statement, "And the tear on your sleeve comes from the pogrom of Kishinev"?

3. What is meant by the statement that the Jewish political radicals were looking for a particularly attractive excuse to escape Judaism by becoming a part of something larger, a universal cause?

4. Why do you think these young Jewish radicals needed an excuse? Why didn't they simply escape?

5. In what sense was Shadrach Cohen not a "real" American according to his sons? How would you sum up their definition of being an American?

A THREE-WAY DISCUSSION*

It is the turn of the century. Three young Jews sit together in the local cafe of a small Russian town, passionately arguing with one another. Each has chosen a different avenue of escape from the misery of Jewish existence in Russia and defends his or her choice with fervor and conviction. There is the Zionist (who shall be referred to as Z), the political radical (R), and the prospective immigrant to the United States (I).

On the basis of what you know about these three avenues of escape, determine in each of the following statements who is likely to be arguing with whom. For example, "Granted, you will have a measure of political freedom and economic opportunity now, but what about roots and heritage and a country of your own? What about your children?" This statement could only have been made by the Zionist, concerned with roots and heritage, to the prospective American, about to gain a measure of political freedom and economic opportunity in the very near future.

1. "You call yourself an idealist? I call you a parochial, narrowminded nationalist." _____ to _____

2. "Your head is full of utopian pipe dreams. Universalism and international brotherhood, indeed! Face facts! Accept reality! What's important is physical safety, political security, and making a decent living for your family." _____ to _____

3. "Maybe you'll have it good for a while. But remember the Golden Age of Spain ended with the Spanish Inquisition. The Jew in someone else's land will always be a stranger—a helpless, haunted, forever uncertain minority." _____ to _____

4. "Maybe I agree with you in principle. But in practical terms, and in the foreseeable future, you'll be trading one kind of misery for another: malaria and marauders can be just as deadly and dangerous as a pogrom; hunger is hunger, whether it is suffered out of necessity or in the name of a noble aim."_____ to _____

5. "You're kidding yourself if you think that you can merge with the masses and define yourself in international terms. Maybe you'll forget who you are, but they won't. Your way leads to losing oneself; my way leads to finding oneself. Your ideals demand that you negate your identity; my ideals allow me to affirm my identity."_____ to _____

PINPOINTING MOTIVES

Complete the following sentences, which could have been made by Russian Jews embarking upon any of the three avenues of escape.

1. I am going to America because

_____

_____

2. I have become a political revolutionary because

_____

_____

3. I am a Zionist because

_____

_____

Chapter Seven

The Power of Ideas

A SEARCH FOR UNDERSTANDING*

The paragraph below briefly touches upon some of the highlights of Chapter Seven, "The Power of Ideas." Fill in the blank spaces, taking words directly from the text when appropriate.

Lilienblum was moved to embrace Jewish nationalism because of

having personally witnessed a _____. This experience per-

suaded him that the Jewish people would always be _____

until they had a land of their own. He was particularly shocked by the par-

ticipation of _____ in these riots; if they, too,
were capable of anti-Semitic actions, he felt, all hope was lost for Jews living
in Russia. Pinsker shared Lilienblum's shock and despair, and in line
with his profession, pronounced anti-Semitism an

_____ and wrote a pamphlet, _____

_____

elaborating upon his ideas. This work, though rejected by a number of
established Jewish leaders, was received enthusiastically by members of

_____, who in turn convinced Pinsker that

_____ was the only country in which a Jewish homeland
would truly take root. This idea was set forth in the works of Bialik, who

would later be known as Israel's _____ because he was

able to express the Jewish _____ with such force and eloquence.

THE MAKING OF A ZIONIST

This chapter focuses upon the insights and longings that propelled young
Eastern European Jews into the orbit of Zionism during the 1880's.
Imagine that you are a member of the Lovers of Zion at that time, and are
writing a brief note to a friend to explain why you have become so involved.

Which elements of your experience have combined to persuade you that Zionism is the answer to the problems of the Jewish people?

REASONS BEHIND THE BELIEFS

This chapter features a number of beliefs about the nature of the Jewish experience—past, present, and future. In a sentence or two, point out what you think are the most likely reasons behind the following beliefs:

1. Pinsker's belief that anti-Semitism is an incurable disease

   _____

   _____

   _____

2. Lilienblum's belief that "aliens we are and aliens we shall remain"

   _____

   _____

   _____

3. Pinsker's and Lilienblum's shared disillusion over anti-Semitic attitudes and actions of Russian intellectuals, which led them to conclude that there was no hopeful future for Diaspora Jewry (Why was this perception of the "cultured" Russians particularly shattering?)

   _____

   _____

4. Rabbi Jellinek's belief that Jewish national rebirth was a joke, an outright impossibility

_____

_____

_____

5. Bialik's belief in the redeeming glory of the land of Israel

_____

_____

_____

WHO SAID WHAT? *

Lilienblum, Pinsker, and Bialik were similar in their belief that the only real remedy for Jewish suffering was a national rebirth in the land of Israel. Yet each man had a distinctive set of experiences, manner of expression, and personal outlook. On the basis of what you have read, figure out who might have made each of the following statements. Designate your choice by placing the first initial of the last name (L, P, B) in the brackets to the right of the statement. Also include another prominent Jewish personality of the day, Rabbi Adolf Jellinek (J).

1. It's like a great big generation gap. The youth listen, while their elders, including those of great learning and influence, dismiss me as a dreamer and a clown. [   ]

2. I was a total innocent for nearly forty years. Only now am I beginning to see and understand the world beyond. [   ]

3. My work has two major themes: one is a record of suffering and despair; the other, a vision of hope beyond every reasonable expectation. [   ]

4. In the best of circumstances, we are outsiders, and we had better face the fact that this situation is not about to change. [   ]

5. Let's deal with life as it really is, and not lose ourselves in impossible dreams. Indulging in these illusions does not help our people; in truth, it only makes matters worse by letting them down. [   ]

6. You say you learned a lot from me? Allow me to return the compliment; I've learned at least as much from you. I feel like an architect with a blueprint; you have shown me the location where we must break ground and begin building. [   ]

7. Yehudah HaLevi wrote: "My heart is in the East." I think I know how he felt. The Israel that I long for is the Israel of my heart. My dreams are rooted in a reality that goes well beyond the grim facts of today. It

reaches back to ancient times and extends into a future that we will fashion from these longings, and create with our own hands. [   ]

8. Look, I've had every advantage that this society has to offer, and I tell you that the Jews have no future here. All my life, I've been waiting for things to get better. They haven't. And they never will. [   ]

YIDDISH HUMOR *

Humor was a basic ingredient in the culture of Eastern European Jewry. It rippled through an atmosphere of unrelieved poverty, uncertainty, and violence, relentlessly ferreting out life's absurdities and inducing a smile or two in the process. Below are several unhumorous descriptions of the way things might have looked to inhabitants of a late nineteenth-century shtetl. Choose the sample (or samples) of Yiddish humor (text, page 48) that you think best sums up each description.

1. No matter what he does and which way he turns, he is dogged by bad luck

2. Life is very difficult; however, we have no choice but to carry on

3. After everything I've done, all the work and worry of raising them, this is the thanks I get

4. That old miser has never parted with a penny unnecessarily in his life. He has never helped anyone, not even members of his family. What pleasure he gets from it God only knows

5. All the religious preaching in the world does nothing to prevent poverty, injustice, and inequality. The distance between the haves and have-nots remains as great as ever

43

Chapter Eight

Founding Fathers

A SEARCH FOR UNDERSTANDING*

---

1. Which of the following descriptions can *not* be applied to the first pioneers who settled in Palestine? (Circle one.)

   a. Idealistic   b. Dedicated to physical labor on the land   c. Hampered by bureaucracy   d. Opposed by fellow Jews   e. Prepared for every problem that came their way

2. Which city was *not* considered one of the four holy cities? (Circle one.)

   a. Jerusalem   b. Jaffa   c. Safed   d. Tiberius   e. Hebron

3. Match the words in the left column with their meanings in the right column.

      a. Ḥalukah   _____ A donation box, placed permanently in many Jewish homes, whose contents helped support the Jewish community living in Palestine

      b. Shliḥim   _____ The Holy Land, the land of Israel

      c. Pushka   _____ The system of distributing or sharing funds from abroad for the support of religious Jews living in Palestine

      d. Eretz HaKedoshah   _____ "Messengers," or representatives sent by the Jewish community in Palestine to Jewish communities abroad for purposes of raising money

4. True or false? The Biluim were the first Jews to work at farming in Israel since the destruction of the Second Commonwealth.
   T [ ] F [ ]

44

5. True or false? The Biluim found the entire land desolate, neglected, and malaria-infested. T [ ] F [ ]

6. The first Zionist colonists and the Orthodox Jewish community clearly did not get along with one another. This was not primarily a clash of personalities, but of principles. Briefly summarize the main accusations that each group leveled at the other.

    a. Orthodox Jews to Zionist colonists _____

    _____

    _____

    b. Zionist colonists to Orthodox Jews _____

    _____

    _____

A BILU DIARY

The aim here is to consider the thoughts and feelings of the young pioneers as they undertook what may have been the greatest adventure of their lives. In the space below, compose an excerpt from the diary of one of the Bilu colonists. If your interests run in directions other than straight narrative, compose a drawing, a poem, a dramatic dialogue, etc. Experiences might include leaving home; arriving in Jaffa; trading at one of the bazaars; getting a permit (for whatever purpose) from the Turkish authorities; traveling around the country; an evening in an Arab village; an encounter with a group of Orthodox Jews; the first day of work—fatigue, blisters, exhilaration, discouragement, and all points between; coping with hardship and illness; a meeting of the group. Be as creative as you wish but take your cues from the text, which serves as a factual reference.

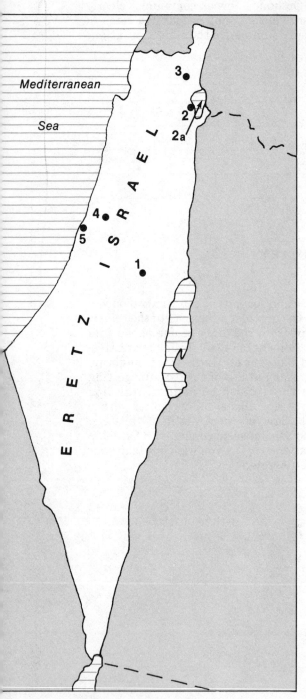

Each of the sites described below is a place that the Biluim either knew about or visited when they immigrated to Palestine in the 1880's. The descriptions include something mentioned in the text and a related fact or two. On the map, fill in the correct name of the place being discussed. The numbers on the map correspond to the numbers next to the descriptions below.

1. The capital of modern Israel, one of the four holy cities, that has been called the "City of David."

2. Another holy city, with a Roman name, located on the banks of a famous lake which is sometimes called the Sea of the Galilee. (Fill in the name of that lake on site 2a.)

3. This holy city, in a high mountain region, has had Jews living in it through all the years of exile. It is noted as a center of Jewish learning and mysticism, and today has among its many exotic inhabitants a sizable colony of artists.

4. The first modern Jewish settlement, today a flourishing city near Tel Aviv, whose name expresses the feelings and dreams of the Biluim.

5. An ancient city that later became a famous seaport and trading center. To the Biluim, it represented the first tangible encounter with the land of their forefathers.

FIND THE QUOTATION

The Bilu Manifesto expressed some of the key ideas of the first Zionist colonists (text, page 54). The statements below spell out several points made by the Manifesto. In the blank space that follows each statement, fill in the specific excerpt (a passage or a sentence from the actual paragraph) that it represents.

1. The claim of the Jewish people to the land of Israel dates back to ancient times.

   _____

2. The land of Israel is of vital importance to all Jews, and not just to those who choose to settle there.

   _____

3. There are all kinds of political realities that have to be accepted in the process of achieving the Zionist dream; at times compromise is necessary — half a loaf is better than none at all.

   _____

4. The roots of the Jewish people in Israel are spiritual as well as historical.

   _____

PIONEERING HASSLES

If the first Zionist pioneers had possessed a contemporary American colloquial vocabulary, one word that might have enjoyed frequent usage would be "hassle." These young people — few in number, lacking resources other than their own ingenuity and stubborn will — had made a lonely decision in a world that knew little and cared less about their aims and ideals. And so they were hassled time and again by an assortment of obstacles — people, natural elements, circumstances, etc. — that had to be coped with along the way. Listed below is a selection of likely sources of hassles. In the spaces following each choice, briefly discuss the kinds of trouble that they might have caused the pioneers.

1. Parents

   _____

   _____

2. Personnel on board ship (to Palestine)

_____

_____

3. A Turkish immigration official

_____

_____

4. A Jaffa merchant

_____

_____

5. The climate

_____

_____

6. The land

_____

_____

7. Local Arabs

_____

_____

8. Orthodox Jews

_____

_____

POSITIVE FACTORS

There were factors that strengthened the pioneers' determination to remain and create a life for themselves in the land of their ancestors. Oddly enough, in certain instances the plus and minus factors stemmed from the same source. In the spaces below, briefly discuss what you think might have been the positive aspects of each factor.

1. Memories of the old country

_____

_____

2. A sense of shared purpose and identity

_____

_____

3. The land (which, viewed in one light, might have proved a source of end-less problems and discouragement, in another light is a challenge and an inspiration)

_____

_____

4. Their strong Zionist background

_____

_____

WORD SCRAMBLE*

Unscramble the following words, each of which is related to the experiences of the Biluim. Then sort out the letters within the circles to make a word that expresses a fundamental Zionist aim.

1. **Fajaf**

2. **Mirgfan**

3. **Disimela**

4. **Eneirop**

Chapter Nine

The First Aliyah

MOTIVATIONS *

The Biluim immigrated to Palestine for a variety of similar reasons. However, each of the characters discussed in the text had at least one distinctive motivation that brought him to this land, a motivation that set him apart from his fellow settlers. Match each motivation described below with the character who harbored it. Also included is the name of one Jew who did not actually settle in Palestine, but was nevertheless deeply involved with the process of colonization.

1. He wanted to see if Jewish farmers could really and truly succeed in Palestine.

2. He believed that the national rebirth of the Jewish people depended upon the revival of an authentic Jewish culture

3. He would not suffer the insults, degradation, and second-class citizenship heaped upon Russian Jews

4. He came to the conclusion that Jews would never be accepted into Gentile society and would always be victims of anti-Semitism in one form or another

_____ Salman Levontin

_____ Joseph Feinberg

_____ Eliezer Ben Yehudah

_____ Baron Edmond de Rothschild

PLACES ON THE MAP *

The numbers on the map opposite correspond to the numbers before the descriptions that follow. Each of these descriptions pinpoints a location either settled or visited by the Biluim. On the basis of these descriptions, fill in the names next to the numbers on the map.

1. An abandoned agricultural colony that was resettled by the Biluim.

2. A colony at the ridge of a famous Israeli mountain that is written about in the biblical account of the prophet Elijah.

3. The name of this colony is derived from a passage in Isaiah.

4. It took a long time and physical hardship to reach the location of this colony high in the mountains of Safed.

5. In its first stages, this colony was a breeding ground for disease and bore witness to a number of tragedies among the pioneers.

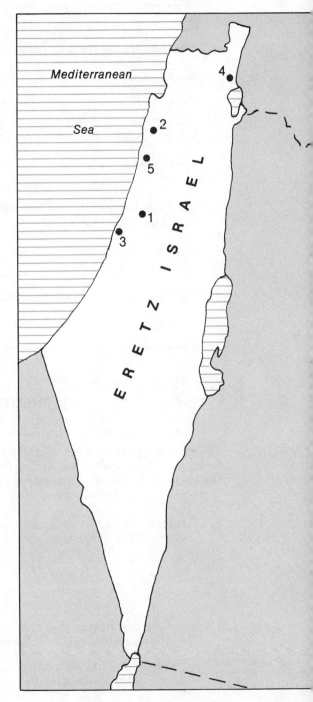

ISSUES IN DEPTH

Support each of the general statements below with a specific reference to, or a quotation from, the text.

1. Pogroms were sometimes carried out with official approval.

_____

_____

_____

2. Many of the early pioneers turned their backs on money, status, and career in favor of their Zionist ideals.

_____

_____

_____

51

3. The Biluim suffered many hardships in the process of trying to strike roots in Palestine.

_____

_____

4. The Biluim were fiercely, passionately, devoted to their cause.

_____

_____

5. Eliezer Ben Yehudah could be described as a dedicated fanatic, who helped change the course of Jewish history.

_____

_____

6. Baron de Rothschild had his own strong ideas about what kind of life the Biluim should live in Palestine.

_____

_____

7. The Biluim had their fair share of doubt, disenchantment, and despair.

_____

_____

PHOTO STUDY

The photographs on pages 65 and 68 give us some idea of what the land of Israel must have looked like during the early years of Zionist settlement. On the basis of the content of these photographs and their accompanying captions, answer the following questions.

1. Point out at least two specific problems of land reclamation that are suggested by the photographs.

2. Circle the description that can *not* be applied to the following sentence: The hills surrounding the Huleh were

    a. Rocky   b. Uninhabited   c. Uncultivated   d. Treeless
    e. Incapable of sustaining life   f. Exposed to the elements

3. The early accounts of the pioneers are full of references to dangers and discomforts that they constantly faced. What sources of potential danger and discomfort can you find in these two photographs?

_____

_____

4. Transforming the Huleh region from malaria-infested swamps into flourishing farmland was a striking example of imagination and hard work overcoming the elements. Similar examples on a more modest scale can be found in the photograph of Tel Aviv. How did the pioneers deal with the following obstacles?

a. A lack of housing facilities _____

_____

b. An absence of paved roads _____

_____

c. Travel and transportation problems _____

_____

5. Tel Aviv in 1921 was in its infancy. There were many limitations, but many opportunities as well. Among the following occupations, which do you think offered a person the chance to make a living, and which were impractical in terms of the setting of 1921? Fill in the spaces after each occupation with either a P (positive prospects) or an N (negative prospects).

a. Bricklayer   [ ]   f. Lawyer   [ ]
b. Farmer   [ ]   g. Doctor   [ ]
c. Carpenter   [ ]   h. Clothier   [ ]
d. Mechanic   [ ]   i. Well digger   [ ]
e. Road builder   [ ]   j. Engineer   [ ]

MEANINGS

In a sentence or two, explain what Edmond Fleg meant when he stated,

1. "I am a Jew because the faith of Israel demands of me no abdication of the mind. . ."

_____

_____

2. "I am a Jew because in every place where suffering weeps, the Jew weeps. . ."

_____

_____

3. "I am a Jew because at every time when despair cries out, the Jew hopes. . ."

_____

_____

4. "I am a Jew because the word of Israel is the oldest and the newest. . ."

_____

_____

5. How does the creation of a modern Jewish state show that "when despair cries out, the Jew hopes"?

_____

_____

FAMILY RELATIONSHIPS *

You do not have to know Hebrew well to try your hand at this activity. A minimal knowledge of the language is sufficient. Below is a list of Hebrew words and their translation. Rearrange them into their proper families, represented by the lined circles. (The root letters will give you the necessary clues.) Each section is large enough to write one Hebrew word and its English translation underneath.

מַעֲבָר   תַּהֲלִיךְ   סִדוּר   עוֹבֵר   הוֹלֵךְ   סֵדֶר   סֵפֶר   מַהֲלָךְ

סוֹפֵר   סַדְרָן   הֲלָכָה   עֵבֶר   סִפְרִיָה   הָעֲבָרָה

מִסְדָּר   בֵּית־סֵפֶר

Translation (in scrambled order):

prayerbook; process; school; transfer; transition; library; law; organizer; go; author; journey; formation (or parade); order; side; book; pass

54

For example:

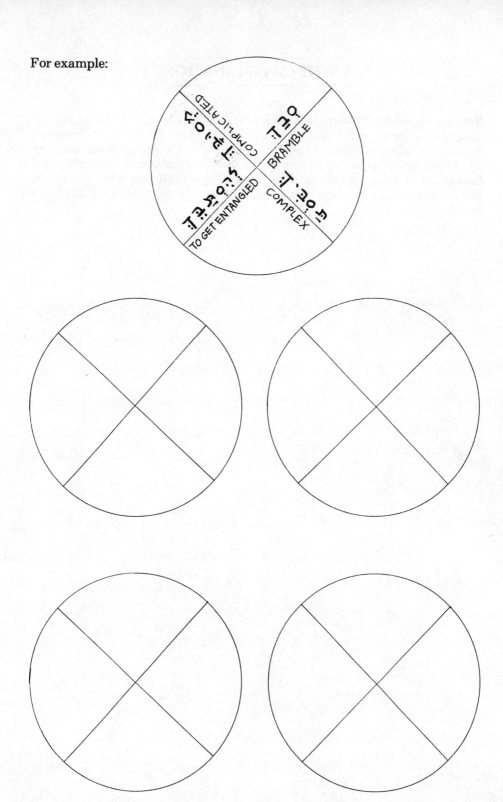

A NOTE OF EXPLANATION

You are Baron de Rothschild's assistant, and it is your job to handle all complaints, large and small. You receive a letter from an exasperated colonist in Palestine, seething with outrage at the Baron's demand that the Biluim observe Orthodox customs and laws, regardless of their personal beliefs, and despite the fact that the Baron himself is hardly what one would call an observant Jew. How would you answer the colonist, explaining the Baron's position?

Unit Three
From Dream to Reality
1905 – 1948

Chapter Ten

Political and Literary Beginnings

PINPOINT THE OUTSIDER *

Under each of the following numbers, one of the lettered statements does not belong. Pinpoint the outsider, and briefly explain the reason for your selection.

1. Herzl became a Zionist because

   a. He believed that anti-Semitism would always be a fact of Jewish life in the Diaspora
   b. He believed that the national homelessness of the Jewish people, along with their status as a minority, made them inevitable candidates for persecution
   c. He believed that once the Jews were a "normal" people with a state of their own, anti-Semitism would eventually disappear
   d. He believed that the fact that the Jewish people were able to remain religiously and culturally intact (and apart from other peoples) for 2000 years entitled them to a state of their own
   e. He was persuaded by the Dreyfus Affair and its aftermath that the Jews were in permanent danger even in enlightened (in terms of laws, official attitudes, etc.) societies

2. Herzl's contributions included

   a. The creation of an organizational structure for modern Zionism
   b. The introduction of the idea that the Jews were a nation as well as a religious group
   c. The establishment of a Zionist movement of international scope
   d. Propelling Zionist aspirations into the arena of politics and diplomacy

e. Infecting his contemporaries with his passion, enthusiasm, and belief in the eventual realization of the Zionist dream

3. Herzl might be described as

   a. An accomplished writer
   b. A man of action
   c. A man consumed by a dream
   d. A charismatic leader
   e. A man who thoroughly understood Judaism and the Jewish people

4. The Dreyfus Affair

   a. Tapped deep reservoirs of anti-Jewish feeling in France
   b. Pointed up the distance between official policy and popular attitudes in an "enlightened" country
   c. Was a conspiracy hatched by anti-Semites to demonstrate that French Jews were subversive outsiders, and should not be regarded as citizens and patriots
   d. Was a classic example of "guilt by generalization"
   e. Shattered the illusions of a number of Western Jews who believed that their place and future in European society was secure

5. The Second Aliyah

   a. Produced some of Israel's greatest leaders
   b. Defined itself in terms of principles of social revolution
   c. Cut itself off completely from Jewish communities in the Diaspora
   d. Found itself in ideological opposition to the Bilu settlers in several areas
   e. Proved to be adept at practical politics, as well as at the formulation of principles and ideals

EVENTS AND EFFECTS *

Match the events listed in the left column with the long range effects listed in the right column.

1. The Dreyfus Affair

   _____ Injected new life, hope, and idealism into the process of Zionist settlement

2. Herzl's appearance on the Zionist scene

   _____ Channeled Zionist aspirations and ideals into a structure of defined programs and institutions

3. The publication of *The Jewish State*

   _____ Convinced Herzl that anti-Semitism would remain an active factor even in supposedly enlightened countries, and that the only valid answer to this problem was for the Jewish people to have a state of their own

4. The creation of the World Zionist Organization

   _____ Gave the ideology of political revolution within Zionism the framework of a political party with international ties

5. The arrival of the Second Aliyah in Palestine

   _____ Was a major breakthrough in the communication of the Zionist idea to the Jewish world at large

6. The establishment of Poale Zion

   _____ Dramatized Zionist aspirations, and mobilized Jews the world over to work actively toward their realization

ISSUES IN DEPTH

Theodor Herzl and the members of the Second Aliyah (in which David Ben-Gurion was a key leader) were makers and movers of history. They responded to oppressive and dangerous forces in their lives by creating a set of hopeful new realities.

The following statements are general descriptions of the character and achievements of these leaders. In the spaces below each statement, elaborate upon these descriptions with specific references to, or a brief quotation from, the text that illustrate how Herzl, Ben-Gurion, and other early Zionist leaders were able to make history happen (e.g., General statement: Theodor Herzl was a writer of great power and clarity. Specific statement: Theodor Herzl's pamphlet *The Jewish State* profoundly influenced the thinking of young Eastern European Jews.)

1. Herzl's organizational genius gave the Zionist dream substance and direction.

_____

_____

_____

2. Herzl's Zionist vision was a study in extremes: extreme pessimism about the future of Diaspora Jewry; extreme optimism about the situation of Jews once they had a state of their own.

_____

_____

_____

3. Herzl understood that Zionist aims would only be achieved by entering the arena of diplomacy and power politics.

_____

_____

_____

4. Herzl instilled in his fellow Zionists a belief in themselves, and in their goals.

_____

_____

_____

5. The members of the Second Aliyah saw nationalism not as an end in itself, but as a framework within which their ideas might be put to work.

_____

_____

_____

61

6. Idealists though they were, the pioneers of the Second Aliyah proved to be able and farseeing practical politicians.

_____

_____

_____

HISTORY'S HEADLINES*

1. To which event or situation discussed in the chapter does each of the news headlines below refer?

   a. CONVICTED NOVELIST FLEES COUNTRY!

   b. SUSPECTED TRAITORS FIRED FROM JOBS!

   c. NEW BOOK STIRS JEWISH YOUTH!

   d. NEWCOMERS CLASH WITH OLD-TIMERS OVER 'MATTERS OF PRINCIPLE!'

   e. REBELLIOUS YOUTH'S PARTING SHOT: 'I'M NOT LEAVING HOME; I'M GOING HOME!'

   f. DELEGATES DECLARE: 'A FAMOUS FIRST!'

   g. EX-DEVIL'S ISLANDER DECORATED!

   h. FAMILY SPLITS! BROTHERS LEAVE COUNTRY, PURSUE THEIR DESTINIES 6000 MILES APART!

2. Make up news headlines to describe the following:

   a. Herzl's shock at witnessing the Dreyfus trial and its aftermath

   _____

   b. Herzl's efforts to negotiate with the Turkish sultan and the British government for a charter permitting Jewish settlement in Palestine

   _____

   c. The arrest of the alleged traitor Alfred Dreyfus _____

   _____

   d. Rumors of an army cover-up (of the Dreyfus Affair) at the highest levels _____

   _____

   e. The arrival of a group of Second Aliyah pioneers at the port of Jaffa

   _____

REASONS

In a sentence or two, complete each of the following statements:

1. Theodor Herzl was shocked by the Dreyfus trial because

   _____

   _____

2. More than 1.5 million Jews left Russia between 1905 and 1914 because

   _____

   _____

3. The pioneers of the Second Aliyah refused to hire Arab labor because

   _____

   _____

4. The Dreyfus Affair triggered a wave of anti-Semitism in France because

   _____

   _____

5. Herzl established the World Zionist Organization because

_____

_____

6. Ben-Gurion declared that galut meant political and cultural dependence for the Jewish people because

_____

_____

and that they would only achieve true independence in their own homeland because

_____

_____

Chapter Eleven

Beggars with Dreams

TRUE OR FALSE, AND WHY? *

What were the pioneers of the Second Aliyah like? Which elements of background, character, and outlook propelled them into a way of life marked by distant dreams, daily frustrations, and a seemingly endless assortment of dangers? The statements below are possible descriptions of the Second Aliyah. Some are true, some are false; mark them accordingly in the brackets that follow, and on the next line briefly explain the reason for your choice.

1. The members of the Second Aliyah were passionate idealists.
    T [   ] F [   ]

    _____

2. Discouragement and despair were virtually unknown within their ranks. T [   ] F [   ]

    _____

3. In some ways, the early pioneers could be called fanatics. T [   ] F [   ]

    _____

4. The Second Aliyah was committed to a cultural, as well as a political, rebirth of the Jewish nation. T [   ] F [   ]

    _____

    _____

5. The pioneers believed that physical labor on the land was a necessary evil, a series of dirty jobs that had to be done if they were to realize their dreams. T [   ] F [   ]

    _____

    _____

6. The life-style of the pioneers was marked by discipline and dedication.
    T [   ] F [   ]

    _____

THE LANGUAGE OF IDEALISM *

Hebrew has a number of special terms that reflect the idealism of the early pioneers. Match the Hebrew word in the left column with the statement in the right column that best expresses its meaning.

1. Ḥalutz

_____ He has not just taught me a skill or given me a body of knowledge; he has instilled in me a set of values upon which I hope to build my life.

2. Aliyah

_____ I have never felt such a sense of personal satisfaction, of inner meaning, as I have working with these people, digging up this land, bearing witness to the birth of a new field, or laying the foundations of a building.

3. Madrich

_____ They don't talk principles and ideals — they live them, totally; that is why so many of the people who have known them come away inspired to do the same.

4. Hagshamah

_____ The significance of our move is not geographical, but spiritual; our purpose is not simply to be transplanted, but to be transformed.

5. Dugmah ḥinuchit

_____ We have staked out the future as our special territory; we can best honor the old, that is the essence of history and tradition, by working to create something new on the soil of our homeland.

IMPRESSIONS

The year is 1913. You have just visited one of the farming communities established by the members of the Second Aliyah. Describe a likely scene from a typical day in the life of these pioneers. You might focus upon any one of the following: working in the fields; greeting a new group of pioneers; dancing and celebrating after work; a conversation with one or several Second Aliyahniks who tell you why they came to Palestine and what they hope the future will bring; an argument over whether Hebrew should be used at all times, as opposed to relaxing every once in a while with Yiddish or Russian; trying to talk several discouraged members out of pulling up stakes and returning to Russia; a visit with A. D. Gordon; whatever likely scene happens to strike your imagination.

A TV INTERVIEW

You are a Second Aliyah ḥalutz and have been asked to do a TV interview (there is a bit of a time warp involved because television has not yet been invented, but never mind,) to clarify for the viewing audience a number of questions about the venture that you have undertaken. Remember you are on TV and must communicate briefly, simply, and memorably, who you are and what you are about.

1. What made you embark upon this adventure in the first place?

2. There are so many odds stacked against you. Why are you so sure that you will succeed?

3. The members of the Second Aliyah can hardly be described as orthodox Jews. Yet you are constantly described in religious terms, in the sense of possessing a strong, unshakable faith. A faith in what, and why?

4. Some people refer to you as fanatics. For example, you refuse to speak to one another in any language but Hebrew, despite the fact that most of you are not fluent Hebraists, and have to twist your tongues and break your teeth to make yourselves understood. Why do you torture yourselves so?

5. What does this fellow A. D. Gordon, who has become something of a living legend, mean when he says, "not labor to make a living, not work as a deed of charity, but work for life itself"?

6. You ḥalutzim spurn what most people work all of their lives to attain: material comfort, a high standard of living, expensive clothes,

leisure time, comfort, and pleasure. What is it that you are looking for in life? And how do you define happiness?

ATTITUDES AND VALUES

In each of the following , draw one circle around the letter whose phrase comes closest to expressing an attitude or value of the Second Aliyahniks. Then, draw two circles around the word that comes closest to expressing your own attitude or value. If they happen to be the same, draw three circles.

1. Physical comfort should be

   a. Ignored   b. Rejected out of hand as a matter of principle   c. Considered nice, but hardly necessary   d. Actively pursued

2. Financial security is

   a. An aim of utmost importance   b. Irrelevant   c. A desirable fringe benefit   d. An illusion   e. A threat to higher ideals

3. Success means

   a. Money   b. Professional achievement   c. Getting along well with family and friends d. Being a just, fair, and compassionate individual e. Devoting your life to an ideal in which you believe   f. Being yourself

4. The State of Israel is

   a. A haven for persecuted Jews   b. An interesting place to visit c. A Jewish country, which deserves the affection, support, and loyalty of Jews everywhere   d. Of vital interest to all Jews and, therefore, comes first in terms of personal involvement and commitment

5. The future is

   a. Nothing more than a replay of the past   b. A depressing prospect c. Largely a matter of circumstances and luck, factors over which there is little or no control   d. A time of opportunity for those who know how to recognize it and take advantage of it   e. A framework for creative innovation, in which people can give shape and direction to their dreams

6. Jewish life outside of Israel

   a. Is eventually doomed to extinction, either by hostile forces from without, or by a process of spiritual and cultural erosion (assimilation) from within   b. Is unhealthy and unnatural   c. Is a question of running furiously to stay in place   d. Offers many channels of Jewish creativity and fulfillment

7. Anti-Semitism

   a. Is, in Pinsker's words, an "incurable disease"   b. Directly threatens Jews today   c. Will gradually disappear in the course of time   d. Is a problem that can be overcome by education, communication, and logic

PIONEERING PRINCIPLES

The members of the Second Aliyah have been described as individuals of deep and unwavering faith. They passionately believed in the cause that they served, and in their ability to realize its aims. Their commitment to work on the soil of Israel was called "the religion of labor," a blend of discipline, dedication, and poetic vision. What, precisely, were the principles in which they believed so profoundly? Using the text as a reference, complete the statements below, which might well have been made by any member of the Second Aliyah.

1. I believe in the Jewish national rebirth because

   _____

   _____

2. I believe that this rebirth must take place in the land of Israel because

   _____

   _____

3. I believe that I must be a part of this process because

   _____

   _____

4. I believe that the act of immigrating to Israel should be called aliyah because

   _____

   _____

5. I believe in speaking Hebrew at all times because

_____

_____

6. I believe that we must create an ideal society in Israel because

_____

_____

7. I believe that I, myself, must do physical labor on the land because

_____

_____

Chapter Twelve

The Second Aliyah

NAMES AND THEIR MEANINGS*

Fit the following names into the appropriate blank spaces in the sentences below (each of which points out the significance of a particular name). If you run into any problems, consult a Hebrew-English dictionary, a map of modern Israel, or the index to *Understanding Israel* (which contains the names of prominent personalities connected with Zionism). Alon Ben Aharon Yizraelah T'nuvah Tikvah Balfouriah Shimshoni Herzliah

1. _____ is derived from the name of one of the great early Zionists.

2. _____ is derived from the name of a famous biblical judge.

3. _____ expresses the hope of a people struggling to create a new nation.

4. _____ is probably derived from the first name of a father of one of the pioneers.

5. _____ is derived from the name of one of Israel's most famous valleys.

6. _____ honors the name of a non-Jewish statesman who played a crucial role in Zionist history.

7. _____ underscores the involvement of the pioneers with agriculture.

8. _____ is the name of a tree that has been associated with the land of Israel since biblical times.

ATTITUDES AND VALUES*

Which of the following attitudes or values is *not* expressed by the names in the exercise you have just completed? (Circle the number before the statement that doesn't belong here.)

1. Kinship with the land

2. The importance of physical labor

3. An awareness and an appreciation of Jewish history

4. A sense of connection with the biblical past

5. A desire to keep alive memories of Jewish ghetto life in the Diaspora

6. Hope for the future of the Jewish people living in a land of their own

YEARNINGS AND NEEDS

Describe in specific terms how the experiences of the Second Aliyah fulfilled the following needs and yearnings of its members:

1. Permanent roots _____

_____

2. Identification with the biblical past _____

_____

3. A new way of life _____

_____

4. A closeness to nature _____

_____

5. Self-expression_____

_____

6. A sense of purpose _____

_____

7. A sense of active, vital Jewish identity _____

_____

FREEDOM FROM, AND FREEDOM TO

Freedom was a major impulse of the pioneering experience. The members of the Second Aliyah were young, strong, thousands of miles from their towns and villages, away from parents, community, traditional authority, and czarist officials. They had a deep sense of release, of liberation. They further realized that "freedom from" (e.g., assorted Diaspora restrictions) was not enough; the persistent exercise of "freedom to" (e.g., create a new social, cultural, and economic framework) was crucial if their actions were to have any lasting meaning.

The statements below are instances of "freedom from" (wherein a Diaspora restriction was lifted because of their move to Palestine) enjoyed by the pioneers. Complete the "freedom to" that you think is appropriate to each of these statements. (For example, *freedom from* the helplessness of minority status; *freedom to* create a strong, just, and healthy society in which they would be a majority).

1. Freedom from the supervision of their parents; freedom to _____

   _____

2. Freedom from the various restraints of Orthodox Judaism which prevailed in Eastern European Jewish life at the time, and which were largely rejected by the pioneers of the Second Aliyah; freedom to

   _____

   _____

3. Freedom from the dangers and anxieties of living in a land where anti-Semitism ran wide and deep and enjoyed official sanction; freedom to

   _____

   _____

4. Freedom from being concerned with other people's attitudes, values, and moods; freedom to _____

   _____

5. Freedom from the demands and goals of a materialistic society; freedom to_____

   _____

6. Freedom from the rootlessness and uncertainty of life in the Diaspora; freedom to_____

   _____

DEFINING PRIORITIES

The pioneers of the Second Aliyah pointedly rejected their life in the Diaspora. They found it spiritually unhealthy, socially and culturally restrictive, politically corrupt, and constantly fraught with danger. They wanted to create a new society in Israel based upon aims, values, and institutions that they believed to be worthy. How would you define your own value priorities? Imagine that you were suddenly given the power to change what you didn't like in your society, and answer the following questions:

1. Name five aspects of your society (or less, if that is all that you can think of) that bother you the most.

   a. _____

   b. _____

   c. _____

   d. _____

   e. _____

2. You have a limited budget to bring about the changes that you would like to see; therefore, list the above problems in what you consider to be the order of their importance.

   a. _____

   b. _____

   c. _____

   d. _____

   e. _____

3. Again, in order of their importance to you, list what you believe to be your community's proudest social achievements.

4. In no more than three sentences, how would you define an ideal society?

5. Think about your answers to the above questions. What do they tell you about your personal values and priorities?

AN ADVERTISING CAMPAIGN

It is unlikely that this would happen (kibbutzim are not in the habit of advertising for members), but for the sake of highlighting some of the key features of kibbutz living, try the following project: You are an executive in an American advertising firm. A particular kibbutz has decided that it wants to attract American members, and toward that end has engaged you to advertise what it has to offer. How would you set forth the advantages of kibbutz living in the following spheres? (In the spaces, simply state, in the form of a memo, what you believe to be its strongest selling points. Don't worry about style. If you feel particularly creative, try making up a catchy slogan for each category.)

1. Education _____

_____

2. Work opportunities _____

_____

3. Health care _____

_____

4. Housing_____

_____

5. Leisure activities_____

_____

6. Old-age benefits _____

_____

7. Community life _____

_____

8. The place of women_____

_____

9. Security and equality_____

_____

10. Which aspects of kibbutz living would you imagine are most likely to

worry or discourage Americans? _____

_____

_____

CONTRASTS

Complete the following:

1. In your community, success is defined as _____
   _____; in the kibbutz,
   _____.

2. In your community, a person's status is determined by _____
   _____; in the kibbutz,
   _____.

3. In your community, the place of money is_____
   _____; in the kibbutz,
   _____.

4. In your community, the position of the elderly is _____
   _____; in the kibbutz,
   _____.

5. In your community, responsibility for the well-being of fellow members
   is _____
   _____; in the kibbutz,
   _____.

Chapter Thirteen

The Ḥalutz

ODD IDEA OUT *

The ḥalutzim came to Palestine with a variety of ideas and ideals that they wanted to put into practice in a Jewish homeland. Each of the following groups of sentences expresses an idea or ideal cherished by the ḥalutzim. Circle the selection that either ignores or negates the statement's meaning.

1. Rejection of the establishment

    a. I am sick and tired of being at the mercy of a stupid, cruel, and openly anti-Semitic government.

    b. I reject the approach of Jewish leaders who tell us to accept our fate, to muddle through as best we can, and wait for the Messiah.

    c. Everyone tells me about my obligations—to my parents, my rabbi, the local authorities, the Jewish people. When I go to Palestine, I'll only be responsible to and for myself; no one will tell me what to do.

    d. All of your middle-class pretensions—the way you talk and dress, the things you buy, your symbols of status and prestige—are meaningless to me. And worse, they fill my mind with false values and goals. I want out of that, which is why I am going to Palestine.

2. Creating an Ideal Community

    a. Everyone will be equal.

    b. A person can fully express his or her individuality as an active, committed member of a group.

    c. To serve as a social, cultural, and moral model for future Jewish settlement.

    d. The individual is nothing; the group, everything.

    e. Great visions can be nourished, and the potential for creativity is virtually unlimited.

3. The meaning of pioneering

    a. The permanent separation of body and spirit.

    b. Discipline and dedication in the name of a higher ideal.

c. A yearning for grass roots democracy and freedom from big government.

d. The courage to reject the old when necessary, and to embrace the new.

CASE IN POINT

Prove each of the statements below with a factual case in point. (e.g., Statement: Christians as well as Jews were aware of the need for a Jewish homeland. Case in point: The Balfour Declaration, issued by the British government in 1917, asserted the right of the Jewish people to create a homeland in Palestine.)

1. To the ḥalutzim politics was more than just an activity, it was a way of life.

   _____

   _____

   _____

2. The ḥalutzim were dreamers and idealists, driven by visions of grand achievement and utopian fulfillment.

   _____

   _____

   _____

3. Commitment to community was a value of primary importance to the early pioneers.

   _____

   _____

   _____

4. External circumstances, as well as inner ideals and aspirations, played a role in the decision of the members of the Third Aliyah to immigrate to Palestine.

   _____

   _____

   _____

5. Anxiety over status and acceptance in their respective Diaspora

societies drove a number of Western Jews to try to undermine the Zionist cause.

_____

_____

_____

6. The experience of the early pioneers demonstrated that rebels against the establishment could be every bit as authoritarian, inflexible, and intolerant as the establishment itself.

    _____

    _____

    _____

7. Yiddish literature in the nineteenth century, far from being a collection of quaint little folktales, was socially aware, morally critical, and tinged with bitterness.

    _____

    _____

    _____

EDITORIAL CRITICISMS *

Zionism sparked a great deal of controversy, not only between those who supported or opposed its aims, but also between those who counted themselves within its framework. There was an abundance of criticism in every direction. No one was exempt. The statements in the right column are editorial criticisms that could have been penned in various Jewish journals and newsletters of the day (1915-1920). The individuals or groups in the left column are candidates for these assorted slings and arrows. Match each critical comment with the individual or group against whom it was most likely to be leveled.

1. British Jewish anti-Zionists   ____ They call themselves rebels against the establishment, but for all of their idealism and noble aspirations, they have precious little patience for the non-conformists in their midst.

2. Russian revolutionaries   ____ They counsel us in the ways of helplessness and

despair. "Accept and adapt," they say, "and make the best of a difficult situation. Bury your heads in holy books, and maybe one day. . . " Well "one day" is now, without any maybe's about it. And we are going to take the future in our own hands and fashion our own destiny!

3. A group of ḥalutzim living on ____ a commune

He is so locked into the old ways that he can not, or will not, learn the lessons of freedom, cannot function in a truly liberated environment.

4. A ḥalutz who could not adapt ____ to the life of the commune

Their fear of "What will the Gentiles say?" drives them to ignore—indeed, to work against—the urgent needs and best interests of the Jewish people.

5. Jewish communal leaders in ____ Eastern Europe

They are selling us pie in the sky about a better world, universal brotherhood, and justice for all. The fact is, the Jew is hated and hurt and killed under every political banner, regardless of ideological principles, or of which group happens to be in control.

A QUIET PROTEST

The quiet protest of Yiddish literature against the frustrations and cruelties of Jewish life in Eastern Europe found a ready audience. The Jews knew the truths contained in these writings. We are several generations removed from what happened then, and so must depend upon these writings for insight and perspective. Each of the themes listed below is expressed in the excerpts taken from the writings of Mendele, Peretz and Sholem Aleichem in the section titled "Quiet Protest." Select the quotation (or quotations) in the text that best fits each theme. At times, a quotation expresses more than one theme, and may, therefore, be used more than once.

1. The reality and seeming permanence of overwhelming poverty

_____

_____

_____

2. Isolation from nature, and from the world at large

_____

_____

_____

3. A mentality that perceives suffering and persecution as a normal state of affairs

_____

_____

_____

4. Skeptical attitudes toward traditional ideas of truth and justice

_____

_____

_____

5. A rejection of the normal life-style of Eastern European Jewry

_____

_____

_____

6. A sense of collective helplessness in the face of forces beyond any Jew's control

_____

_____

_____

THE MEANING OF INDIVIDUALITY

The ḥalutzim of the Third Aliyah were deeply concerned about the question of individuality, particularly within the framework of the special community that they were trying to create. They had very strong ideas about an individual's role in, and relationship to, the community at large. What are your ideas on this subject?

1. An individual is one who _____

    _____

    _____

2. There are very strong pressures in our daily experience that try to compel us to be like everyone else—in effect, to abandon our impulses to individual expression. Can you identify pressures to conform that come from the following sources?

    a. Your friends_____

    _____

    b. Your community _____

    _____

    c. Advertisements _____

    _____

    d. Movies and television _____

    _____

    e. Your own ambitions and needs _____

    _____

3. How do you shape up as an individual? To get some idea, rate yourself on each of the following questions on a scale of 1–10. Ten means that the statement in question describes you 100 percent of the time, 5 means that the statement describes you 50 percent of the time, and so on.

    a. I choose my clothes on the basis of personal taste alone, rather than current fashion. [   ]

    b. When someone expresses an idea, I try to think it through and judge it on its own merit, rather than by what other people say. [   ]

    c. I would defend a position that I believe in, even if it meant my becoming an outcast among my friends. [   ]

    d. I will choose a career on the basis of what I really and truly want to do, rather than considerations of status, prestige, or money. [   ]

    e. I conduct my Jewish life—degree of involvement, nature of commitment, observance of tradition, ties to Israel—solely along lines that I have worked out for myself. They reflect my deepest personal beliefs and values. [   ]

You are your own judge in this little individuality quiz, and your choice of numbers can mean anything you want them to mean. A score of 35 or over, however, can be taken as an indication that you are, or want to be, your own person.

Chapter Fourteen

The Labor Brigade

A SEARCH FOR UNDERSTANDING*

Complete the paragraphs below by inserting the following words in the blank spaces where they apply: within the community   Haganah   pride and prestige   vitality   Hashomer   hired Arab guards   new settlements   Biluim   self-sufficiency   fighting   roads   physical labor   kibbutz   Labor Brigade

_____ was the first official defense agency of the Yishuv, founded in 1907 to help establish _____, and to protect Jewish villages located in heavily populated Arab areas. Those who formed this organization believed that real security for the Jewish settlers would only come from _____ and not from _____. This organization was opposed by the _____, who, among other reasons, doubted the _____ ability of the Jewish quards. Nevertheless, Hashomer endured and effectively protected the growing Jewish community in Palestine until 1920 when it was replaced by the _____.

Just as Hashomer expressed the Zionist yearning for Jewish _____ in matters of defense, so the _____ expressed the desire of the pioneers to rebuild the land of Israel with their own hands. The major task of this group was to create a network of _____ that would connect a number of key locations in Palestine. Being a member of this group was considered a matter of _____ among the ḥalutzim, which reflected the high priority placed upon _____ in those days, a value that flourishes in the _____ and other agricultural communities even today. This value was greatly appreciated by A. D. Gordon, who insisted that it was an essential key to the national _____ of the Jewish people.

ISSUES IN DEPTH

Support the general statements below with specific references to, or quotations from, the text.

1. The ḥalutzim of the Second Aliyah believed that all of the tasks associated with settlement of the land should be done by the Jews themselves.

   _____

   _____

   _____

2. The Biluim did not embrace the value of Jewish self-sufficiency with the same degree of conviction or enthusiasm as the ḥalutzim of the Second Aliyah.

   _____

   _____

   _____

3. The Jewish settlers had good reason to be suspicious of the Arabs in the area.

   _____

   _____

   _____

4. Status and respect on the kibbutz are based upon different values from those that prevail in American society.

   _____

   _____

   _____

5. Physical courage was highly prized by the early Zionist settlers.

   _____

   _____

   _____

MAP STUDY *

The Labor Brigade is noted, among other things, for its achievements in road construction. When the early pioneers arrived in Palestine during the first decades of this century, they found a country physically divided; travel was difficult and dangerous. They sought to unite the land by creating a network of roads, a process that still goes on today. On the map below are a series of such roads, each bordered by two letters that mark the locations that it connects. On the basis of the following information identify these locations by writing their names next to the appropriate letters:

1. **A–B** connects two of Israel's major cities. Both are located on the coastline and have served as seaports.

2. **C-D** connects a major Israeli city, known as the capital of the Negev, whose name goes back to the days of Abraham, with the southern port at the Gulf of Aqaba from which Israeli ships travel to the Red Sea, the Indian Ocean, and Africa.

3. **A-E** connects the above-mentioned (see #1) urban center, Israel's largest city, with the "City of David."

4. **C-F** connects the above-mentioned Negev capital (see #2), which gained a reputation as a rugged frontier town after the creation of the state of Israel, with a city whose name is derived from an ancient biblical site destroyed by God because of the behavior of its inhabitants.

5. **F-G** extends to an ancient mountain fortress overlooking the Dead Sea,

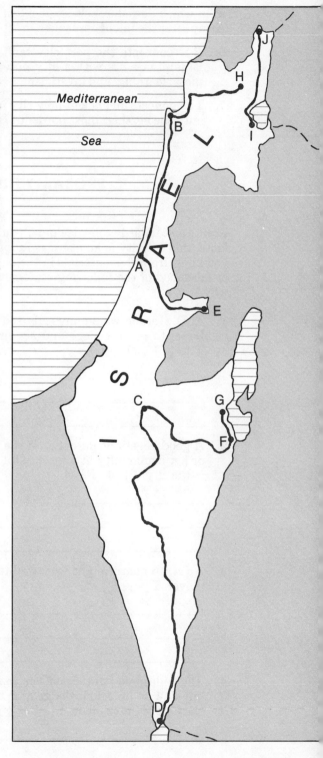

87

from which Jewish rebels made a last stand against the conquering Roman Army after the fall of Jerusalem in 70 c.e.

6. **B-H** connects the port city built upon the "mountain of the prophet Elijah" (see #1) with a city noted for centuries as a center of Jewish piety, learning, and mysticism.

7. **I-J** connects an ancient holy city located on the shores of Lake Kinneret with the northernmost border of Israel proper.

PROBABLY TRUE OR FALSE? *

Unlike a standard true-false quiz, which is based upon reference to specific facts, this activity is an exercise in logical deduction. On the basis of what you know from the materials in the chapter, decide upon the probable truth or falsehood of the following statements, and in a sentence or two, explain why.

1. A. D. Gordon would have advised a young Zionist planning to settle in Israel to go to college and acquire a profession before coming.
   T [　] F [　]

   _____

   _____

   _____

2. A good vegetable gardener in the kibbutz enjoys as much status in his or her community as a successful business or professional person does in the city. T [　] F [　]

   _____

   _____

   _____

3. An Arab guard might very well feel a sense of power over his Bilu employer. T [　] F [　]

   _____

   _____

   _____

4. The widespread anti-Semitism in Russia made it totally impossible for any Jew to be acknowledged, or to secure a position on merit, outside the Pale of Settlement. T [　] F [　]

   _____

5. A member of Hashomer might have declared that learning to fight was not just a matter of necessity, but of the highest Zionist principle. T [ ] F [ ]

_____

_____

6. The ḥalutzim of the Second Aliyah would have welcomed an influx of Jewish businessmen to Palestine as a much-needed shot in the arm to the economy of the Yishuv. T [ ] F [ ]

_____

_____

PHOTO STUDY

Imagine that you have to give a five-minute talk on Hashomer to a group that is familiar with its basic historical background (as presented in the text, pages 100–101), but wants insights into, and impressions of, this first Zionist defense force that go beneath the surface. Your only other source is the photograph that appears on page 101 of the text. What can you derive about the following matters?

1. Weaponry _____

_____

2. Manner of dress and appearance _____

_____

3. Age range of the members _____

_____

4. The role of women _____

_____

Chapter Fifteen

Dreamers of Bittania — A Case Study

WHO (OR WHAT) AM I?*

1. I can be described as a secular holy person. People didn't listen to me; they worshiped me._____

2. On the surface, I can be compared to an early Zionist pioneer. I, too, was adventurous and became a folk hero, but basically I was a loner. The idea of settling down anywhere just made me itch all over. _____

   _____

3. I have been associated with the ideal of freedom for almost as long as there has been a Jewish tradition. _____

   _____

4. I was created in the depths of Jewish tragedy, by enemies of the Jewish people and have been kicking around for some 2000 years. Yet I am a deeply ingrained part of the Jewish experience, and am likely to remain so for a long time to come. Some Zionists have tried to reject me, or to ignore the fact of my existence, but have found that it's not easy; too much of them is tied up in me. _____

5. The settlers of Bittania used my name to describe themselves. I guess it gave them a sense of unity and revolutionary purpose._____

   _____

6. I am the Zionist movement from whose ranks the Bittaniaites came.

   _____

7. I was the activity that served as a springboard for the impassioned out-pourings of the Bittania settlers nearly every evening. I am still widely used today, but in a quieter way, for such purposes as intellectual illumination and ideological discovery. _____

VANTAGE POINTS *

People tend to see things from their own vantage points, and their descriptions are most often colored by their personal interests and beliefs. Therefore, the same experience might come out sounding like two quite different phenomena when characterized by individuals whose life-styles and values happen to clash. Match the descriptions rendered by a critical outsider in the left column, with those of a Bittaniaite in the right column. In the spaces below each statement in the right column, note the people, places, or events that you think are being described.

OUTSIDER

1. A real white elephant. Depressing-looking, rocky, with little progress to show for a lot of work. And although it has an impressive view, that won't make you a living — or a life.

2. I ask you, what was wrong with what they had? Good homes, enough to eat, fine educations — everything that anyone could reasonably hope for.

3. A brainwasher! A hypnotist! A devil who has cast a spell over everyone.

BITTANIAITE

___ We were slaves — to a full belly, to the illusion of security, to the rewards of status and class, and to the lessons that would qualify us as honored, moneyed functionaries of a corrupt system, whose perpetuation was to be our loftiest goal.

_____

_____

___ The most deeply spiritual experience that I ever had, almost religious in character. And never have I known such a feeling of well-being, of inner peace.

_____

_____

___ A true challenge: to make something out of nothing. And think of the history! Every stone has its own story to tell. And by the sweat of our brows and the pain of our bodies, we will restore its ancient glory!

_____

_____

4. This was pure paganism, with ___ A union of the spirit; kindred souls linked forever by shared passion, values and purposes. Our bonds are not accidental. They have been forged by an act of will on the part of every single member of the group.

5. They call it a community. I ___ He has expanded our minds, liberated our emotions, and has made us see and feel and understand as we never have or could have before.

BITTANIA'S MEANING

Imagine that you are a Bittaniaite, whose parents have just visited your commune, and have gone away shocked at what they witnessed. Nothing made sense to them. Everything struck them as extreme, at best, an exercise in youthful self-indulgence that should be brought to an end as quickly as possible. You decide to write them a letter explaining that this is not a fling, but a way of life that is of utmost importance to you. You want to communicate to them, briefly and vividly, the meaning of your community, and the satisfactions that you have found here. How would you do it? What points would you make?

VALUES AND NEEDS

Most observers agree that Bittania was but an exaggerated and intensified reflection of pioneering values and needs. How, then, did the following values and needs of the ḥalutzim find expression in Bittania?

1. Authority (The ḥalutzim had rejected the authority of the Eastern European governments, as well as their own religious leadership.)

    _____

    _____

2. Community _____

    _____

3. Self-expression_____

    _____

4. Passion _____

    _____

5. Nature _____

    _____

6. Discipline _____

    _____

7. Self-esteem _____

    _____

8. A sense of higher purpose _____

    _____

AMERICAN JEWISH VARIATIONS

How are the following values and needs expressed in American Jewish communal life?

1. Connection with the past _____

    _____

2. A sense of Jewish identity _____

    _____

93

3. Ties with Israel _____

_____

4. Responsibility for Jews in less fortunate circumstances _____

_____

_____

5. Commitment to Jewish survival in the future _____

_____

_____

6. Communal and cultural life _____

_____

7. Full acceptance as Americans _____

_____

8. Relevance and modern life-styles _____

_____

WORD SCRAMBLE *

Unscramble the words below. Each of them relates in some way to the experience of Bittania. Then, unscramble the six letters that fall within the circles to make a word that expresses a longing, a vision, shared by every Bittaniaite.

1. **headd**

2. **necumom**

3. **hashi**

4. **sinopas**

5. **shicraticam**

A JEWISH STATE AND A STATE OF JEWS

A distinction has been drawn between a Jewish state and a state of Jews. How would you define the difference between the two concepts? Can you come up with an example that illustrates the difference?

HISTORY AND TRADITION

Berl Katznelson makes the point (page 108) that the past can have a great deal of bearing upon the present and the future. He cites Passover as an example, for its love of freedom and hatred of slavery, a theme that is as crucial to us today as it was to our ancestors in the time of Moses. Choose any one of the following entities, all of which have figured prominently in Jewish history and/or tradition, and show how its values, or its lessons, can be applied to our contemporary lives.

1. The Sabbath   2. The worship of idols   3. False prophets   4. The commandment to honor your father and mother   5. The concept of study for its own sake   6. The story of Hannukah   7. Whatever tradition or event has special meaning to you

Unit Four
The State of Israel

Chapter Sixteen

An Open Wound

A SEARCH FOR UNDERSTANDING *

Chapter Sixteen is filled with important facts that need to be registered and retained. Complete the blank spaces below.

1. Kibbutz Yad Mordechai, founded in _____ by a group of Zionist pioneers who managed to escape the _____, and located south of Ashkelon, an ancient _____ stronghold, stands but a few hundred yards from the _____ _____.

2. Named for _____ _____, the commander of the _____ _____ , Kibbutz Yad Mordechai inscribed its own name in the annals of Jewish heroism by blocking an entire _____ brigade for _____ days, giving Jewish units farther north time to set up a _____ of _____, in effect, saving the infant Jewish state from _____.

3. Hopelessly outnumbered and outgunned, the members of Yad Mordechai lost _____ men, with another 30 wounded. At times they fought the tanks and vehicles with nothing more than _____ _____. Some of the fighters wished to follow the example of the Warsaw Ghetto uprising — that is, by doing battle until the _____ _____ had fallen. Happily, they decided not to do so, and after the War of Independence, lived to see Yad Mordechai _____. The only physical reminder of the battle is a shattered _____ _____.

4. The Warsaw Ghetto uprising came about because the remaining Jews,

some _____ out of an original number of 500,000, were convinced that the Germans planned their ultimate

_____, the real meaning of the Final Solution of the Jewish Problem.

5. This uprising, considered the most dramatic act of Jewish

_____ of World War II, took place, significantly, during the

Jewish holiday of _____, and lasted some _____ days, finally ending only after an all-out German military assault, with the

blowing up of the ghetto _____.

6. Another instance of the "people factor" at work was the construction of

the _____ _____, which effectively put an end to the

siege of _____, whose _____ lines had been cut off by Arab forces. The aim of this project was to bring food, water, and other vital necessities to the besieged city on a regular basis. This they achieved by carving an alternate route through the

_____.

HISTORY'S HEADLINES *

Which events or developments set forth in the chapter might the following news headlines be describing?

1. "DEAD" CITY REBORN; RISES FROM ANCIENT RUINS

2. AUTHORITIES DENY DESTRUCTIVE DESIGNS, STRESS POSITIVE ASPECTS OF RELOCATION

3. TROOPS TAKEN BY SURPRISE; DIDN'T EXPECT CIVILIAN REACTION

4. TEACHER PUNISHED FOR BREAKING THE LAW — ALL STICKS ORDERED CONFISCATED

5. "BREAKTHROUGH AN UPHILL STRUGGLE," WARNS LEADER, "THERE'S A ROCKY ROAD AHEAD!"

6. LEADERSHIP BITTERLY DIVIDED OVER WHAT TO DO. "A GAMBLE FOR SURVIVAL," ASSERTS ONE FACTION. "DEATH INEVITABLE," INSISTS OPPOSITION, "HONOR, OUR ONLY CHOICE!"

7. NEIGHBORS ENTER FRAY; IGNORE PLEAS FOR NONINTERFERENCE

8. SETTLERS STAND THEIR GROUND, REFUSE TO BE BUDGED BY OUTSIDE PRESSURE

ENEMY EDITORIALS *

How would a Nazi or Arab editorial have discussed the above developments (which remain the same here, but in scrambled order)? To which headline does each of the following comments refer? Place the number of the headline in the brackets at the end of each statement.

1. What is most deplorable is that these acts of subversion are committed by so-called intellectuals. [ ]

2. Our armies have heeded the cries of help from our brothers, and have dedicated themselves to a fight to the finish against aggression. [ ]

3. Zionist expansionism, it would seem, knows no limits, and certainly shows no respect for the past. Its latest act of sacrilege has been to defile long-standing landmarks of six civilizations in its frenzy to build, build, build. [ ]

4. The Israelis go to great lengths to portray themselves as underdogs. But it did them no good in the end. Our forces, though vastly outnumbered in men and military equipment, rallied and defeated the enemy in less than a week. [ ]

5. The Jews will do anything, including scaring their fellow Jews to death with dark suspicions, to avoid doing productive labor. [ ]

6. They couldn't, or wouldn't, meet our troops head on and engage in honorable battle. No, they had to sneak in through the back door, so to speak. [ ]

7. "We were just doing our job," the officer told me, "when suddenly, without any warning, they attacked us, murdering and maiming our finest young men." [ ]

8. We would urge those who court anarchy and chaos to heed the warnings

of their wiser fellow Jews: law and order will be upheld at all costs, and by the harshest means at our disposal. [   ]

COUNTERING PROPAGANDA

Israel and the Jewish people in general have been subject to propaganda attacks from enemies who believe that a big lie, or a big smear, if repeated often enough, begins to be accepted. Each of the propaganda statements below can be effectively refuted by a fact or an insight drawn from this chapter. See how you do as a lie detector.

1. The Israelis are colonial parasites, living off the labor of the native Arab population.

    _____

    _____

2. The Israelis have a state today because they initiated a war of aggression against the Arab citizens of Palestine.

    _____

    _____

3. The Jews of Israel were saved from destruction in 1948 by the active intervention of the western powers, and because of their superior technology of weapons.

    _____

    _____

4. Israel came into being as a result of a massive injustice, taking away the homes and towns, fields and industries, of the Arabs.

    _____

    _____

5. One of the major contributing factors to the Holocaust was the fact that the Jews were cowards, and offered no resistance to Nazi terror.

    _____

    _____

6. The Jews in the concentration camps aided and abetted the Nazis by marching to their deaths like sheep to slaughter, saying nothing, doing nothing.

    _____

    _____

101

MOTIVES AND VALUES

Below are some of the motives and values that helped determine the developments described in the chapter. Match the motives and values (sometimes more than one; sometimes the same motive or value will come into play in several instances) with the developments that follow. And if you think that factors other than those on this list deserve to be mentioned, put them down.

a. Honor
b. A perception of no other choice
c. A commitment to national survival
d. The desire for power, prestige, and territory
e. A gamble for life
f. The need to preserve dignity and values in the face of barbarism
g. A sense of connection with the past
h. Distrust of cultural, religious, and ethnic strangers
i. A respect for personal heroism
j. The weight of responsibility for the well-being of fellow Jews, expressed by the policy of proceeding with caution
k. Fear of enemy power
l. A need to identify with the Jewish victims of the Holocaust
m. A "last stand" approach

1. Giving Kibbutz Yad Mordechai its name

   _____

2. The invasion of Israel by neighboring Arab armies

   _____

3. The defense of Yad Mordechai

   _____

4. The desire on the part of some of the kibbutz members to fight and die to the last person

   _____

5. The early decision of Warsaw Ghetto leaders to cooperate with the Germans

   _____

6. The ultimate decision of the Warsaw Ghetto leaders to resist the Germans

   _____

7. The various forms of intellectual and spiritual resistance practiced by the Jews of Europe

---

THE PEOPLE FACTOR

The people factor figured prominently in the Jewish struggle for honor and survival, both in Nazi-occupied Europe, and in Israel at the time of its creation. What inspired these Jews to rise above all normal levels of determination and endurance? Put yourself in their place, and try to see and feel what they might have seen and felt. Set down your perceptions and impressions in the form of a paragraph from a journal, a drawing, a poem, a brief story, or in whichever medium you feel most creative. Personal experiences that you might try to portray include:

1. A debate between opposing factions in the Warsaw Ghetto, as to how to respond to the Nazis
2. Conducting a Hebrew lesson, at great risk, in a concentration camp
3. Attending a secret Bar Mitzvah ceremony in the Warsaw Ghetto
4. A description of the final hours of resistance in the Warsaw Ghetto
5. One of the six days in which the members of Yad Mordechai held out against the Egyptians.
6. Participating in the building of the Burma Road
7. The ceremony marking the rebuilding of Yad Mordechai
8. Looking out past the fields of Yad Mordechai at the refugee camps in the Gaza Strip
9. An appropriate scene of your own choosing

THE MEANING OF SPIRITUAL RESISTANCE

A survivor of the Holocaust is asked the following question by a friend many years later: "I admit, I can't begin to understand what it must have been like during those years, and I certainly don't presume to judge anything that you or your fellow Jews did. But one thing really puzzles me. Why did you go to so much trouble to maintain the semblance of a normal life, when conditions were so cruelly abnormal? What was the point of the concerts and the Bar Mitzvahs and the secret Hebrew classes and the research projects in the face of certain, and in many cases almost immediate, disaster? Why did you spend so much time and energy upon activities that were so obviously futile?" How might such a survivor respond to these questions? What points might be made to explain these activities?

Chapter Seventeen

Yad Mordechai Today

ISSUES IN DEPTH

A community is composed of many elements that are sometimes diverse, and even contradictory. Yad Mordechai is no exception. Its experience is enriched by the need to remember the past and to create a future; by images of death and destruction, and a relentless assertion of the will to live; by dark fears and cautious optimism; by a consciousness of senseless violence and a pride of solid achievement; and finally, by the determination to survive in the face of looming odds in a world that has proved indifferent or even hostile to their fate, and the nagging moral ambivalence that has characterized the settlers' feelings about the refugee camps a few hundred yards away. Flesh out the following general descriptions of the Yad Mordechai experience with specific references (direct quotations, or your summary of pertinent material) from the text.

1. Yad Mordechai is a forward-looking community that is trying to build for the future.

   _____

   _____

2. A member of Yad Mordechai has a variety of occupations from which to choose.

   _____

   _____

3. Yad Mordechai is a pleasant, culturally rewarding place in which to live.

   _____

   _____

4. A settler in Yad Mordechai would find it difficult to ignore the moral issues of the Arab-Israeli conflict, even if he or she were so inclined.

   _____

   _____

5. A young person growing up in Yad Mordechai is not likely to be ignorant of the dramatic, and dangerous, birth pangs of the Jewish state.

    _____

    _____

6. In Yad Mordechai, one is made keenly aware of the fact that Israel is part of the broader canvas of Jewish history, and that it cannot and must not be viewed as an isolated phenomenon.

    _____

    _____

7. Yad Mordechai is living proof that the deepest moral problems have no easy answers.

    _____

    _____

OFFICIAL STATEMENTS *

Official statements are often formulated to place the policies and actions of various governments in the best (or least unfavorable) possible light by talking around, or away from, the issue at hand. It encompasses the ability to rationalize, to speak in generalities, to blunt the edge of urgent or embarrassing questions. To cite but one example, a mayor whose administration has been found to be riddled with corruption might choose either of the following statements:

"I am shocked at these findings. As you know, I have placed myself on the record as fighting for public morality on every level. In line with these principles, I am appointing a blue-ribbon commission to conduct a full-scale investigation of this and other matters of public concern."

"A truly deplorable situation! I think that it goes deeper than any one department, or even any one city. It is a national problem and must be dealt with on national, rather than local, terms. It is a product of Vietnam. And Watergate. And government secrecy. And inflation. And drugs. And crime in the streets. . ."

Each of the offical statements in the right-hand column refers to an event or development (cited in the chapter) in the left-hand column. See if you can match them.

1. An Arab official explaining ____ Recent events prove what
    the intention of his govern-   we have been saying all
    ment to prepare for a second   along. These people cause

round with Israel in defiance of the Arab-Israeli agreements of 1949

trouble wherever they go; nobody wants them. Our policies are simply an honest reflection of international opinion.

2. A British official commenting ____ upon the sinking of the Struma

Our forces have liberated this ancient citadel of faith so cherished by the great religions of the world. And it is our intention to protect its sanctity and the lives of its inhabitants until justice is done.

3. A German official defending ____ his government's policies after boatloads of Jewish refugees could find no port of entry

Our hearts go out to these people, and we sincerely wish them well in their countries of origin. To have let them settle here, however, would have meant going against our own immigration laws which, as you know, have proved to be the mainstay of oppressed peoples everywhere, who come here secure in the knowledge that they will not be persecuted because of race, creed, or color. We pray that every nation learns this lesson before it is too late!

4. A Jordanian official announcing the annexation of the Old City of Jerusalem

Of course we respect agreements, and we desire peace in the area. But peace without honor is just another name for appeasement. And there can be no peace as long as aggression is allowed to flourish. It is our aim to eliminate aggression, thus serving the cause of lasting peace.

5. An American official explaining his country's position after the boat

This attack upon unarmed civilians is inexcusable and tragically demonstrates

bearing 900 Jewish refugees was compelled to return to Europe the barbarism of the enemy, a quality that we have long recognized, which is why we stood up to them and resisted their onslaught virtually alone, while the rest of the world was conquered, quiet, or uncaring.

THE LESSONS OF HISTORY

The members of Yad Mordechai are deeply and intensely involved with Jewish history. They relate to the past not as a shrine to which one must pay homage, but as a guidepost illuminating the present and pointing to the future. What are the lessons to be learned from the following developments of recent Jewish history?

1. The defense of Yad Mordechai

    _____

    _____

2. The situation of the Arab refugees

    _____

    _____

3. The refusal of various countries to allow Jews fleeing from Nazi Germany to enter their borders

    _____

    _____

4. The fact of the European Holocaust

    _____

    _____

5. The absorption of so vast a number of Jewish immigrants to Israel (more than double its total population in 1948) in less than 2-½ decades

    _____

    _____

ODD PERSON, IDEA, OR EVENT OUT *

In each of the statements below, choose the person, idea, event, or other category that you think is out of place, and briefly explain why.

1. Which of the following individuals will probably not be able to put his skill to work at Yad Mordechai?

    a. A carpenter   b. A teacher   c. A farmer   d. A soldier
    e. a bookkeeper   f. A mechanic   g. A librarian   h. A lawyer
    i. An efficiency expert

    _____

    _____

2. Which of the following elements was not a cause, direct or indirect, of the plight of the Arab refugees?

    a. The fears of the Arab inhabitants   b. Israeli military prowess
    c. The ambitions and active intervention of neighboring Arab governments   d. The settlement in Israel of refugees from the Holocaust, and later, from a number of Arab countries   e. The refusal, for various reasons, of the Arab governments to resettle the refugees in their own countries

    _____

    _____

3. Which idea is likely not to figure prominently in the thinking of Yad Mordechai members?

    a. The possible destruction of the Jewish state   b. The mutual sense of connection and commitment between Israelis and other Jews   c. The fear of unemployment   d. The problem of the Palestinians in the Gaza Strip   e. New cultural and economic questions within the kibbutz
    f. Making the next generation aware of recent Jewish history

    _____

    _____

4. Which factor was not responsible for the situation of Jewish refugees' having no place to go?

    a. Nazi concentration camps   b. The bureaucracies of the various governments involved   c. British fear of Arab reaction   d. American internal politics, particularly in light of a growing isolationism
    e. Moral insensitivity   f. Indifference   g. Anti-Semitic attitudes (of both the conscious and subconscious varieties)

    _____

    _____

5. The Arab governments immediately reneged on the agreements of 1949 because

    a. They hoped to destroy Israel in the foreseeable future   b. Their hatred of Israel was too strong to be erased by a treaty   c. They hoped to make peace with Israel from a position of strength, and on their terms   d. They knew that world opinion would neither condemn nor penalize them for their actions   e. They wanted to enhance their prestige by a military victory   f. They still hoped to grab huge chunks of Israeli land for themselves

    _____

    _____

    _____

POINT COUNTERPOINT

Imagine that you are a member of Yad Mordechai. How would you counter the following arguments that might be raised by an Arab refugee living in the Gaza Strip?

1. Forget politics and all the rest. The fact is, you live in land that was once inhabited by me, my family, and my friends.

    _____

    _____

    _____

2. You are an out and out expansionist. Just look at the difference in the size of your kibbutz when you first settled here, and today.

    _____

    _____

    _____

3. You practice religious discrimination as well. Look at your Oriental immigrants. All from Arab lands. You had no qualms about bringing them to Israel, and devoting your time, energy, and resources to integrating them. Why? Because they are Jews, while we are Moslems and Christians.

    _____

    _____

    _____

110

4. You say that you are concerned about our plight. Rubbish! More than 25 years have passed and you have done nothing. Absolutely nothing!

_____

_____

_____

A RESEARCH PROJECT

With so large an infusion of new immigrants, especially those who came from Arab lands, Israel had its work cut out for it in many ways. Make out a checklist of things that had to be done in the process of absorbing these newcomers into the social, cultural, and economic spheres of the country. What do you think were the main problems that were likely to confront the Israelis along the way? Compare your checklist with those of your classmates to see if there is anything that you missed. Then, choose one of the problems or things to do, and find out specifically how the Israelis dealt with it. *Facts About Israel,* issued annually by the government of Israel, and available free of charge at the Israeli Consulate in your area, contains more than enough information on this subject.

Checklist

☐ _____

☐ _____

☐ _____

☐ _____

☐ _____

Specific Problem

Chapter Eighteen

Memories and Reminders

REMEMBERING THE HOLOCAUST *

The Holocaust lies at the center of Israeli consciousness, and is a pivotal event in modern Jewish history. How much do you know about it? The review that follows, which is based upon general knowledge rather than the specific information given in the chapter, attempts to highlight a number of key elements of the Holocaust and World War II, the setting in which it took place. The answers to the questions can be found on page 215.

1. What were the years in which Hitler was in power?

   _____

2. What does the word "Nazi" stand for?

   _____

3. What was the name of the book that Hitler wrote, before coming to power, in which he set forth his political ideology and specific aims?

   _____

4. True or false? The Nazis seized power by overthrowing the duly elected German goverment. T [　] F [　]

5. Which of the following factors did not contribute in some manner to the coming to power of the Nazi party? (Circle one.)

   a. Chaotic economic conditions   b. Widespread discontent and frustration in Germany   c. Chamberlain's policy of appeasement d. Hitler's personality   e. The terms imposed upon Germany after its defeat in World War I

6. What was the name of the German government in power from the end of World War I until the Nazis took over?

   _____

7. By what other name was Nazi Germany known?

   _____

8. Match the names of some of Hitler's top lieutenants, in the left column, with the functions that they performed, in the right column.

    a. Heinrich Himmler   ____ Foreign Minister

    b. Joseph Goebbels   ____ Munitions Minister

    c. Hermann Goering   ____ Head of the elite SS

    d. Joachim von Ribbentrop   ____ In charge of propaganda

    e. Albert Speer   ____ Head of the Luftwaffe (the German Air Force); until the end of World War II, Hitler's designated successor

9. During World War II, Nazi Germany had two major partners, Italy and Japan. Together, they were known as the _____ powers. Their opponents — including, among others, Great Britain, the United States, and the Soviet Union — were called the _____.

10. The respective heads of government in Italy and Japan during World War II were _____ and

_____.

11. The League of Nations, predecessor of the United Nations, lost its claim to legitimacy when it did nothing, and said nothing, about Italy's invasion of _____ in 1935.

12. True or false? World War II began on December 7, 1941, when the Japanese attacked Pearl Harbor. T [   ]   F [   ]

13. A German city that has come to be recognized as a synonym for appeasement, dishonor, and the betrayal of national commitment is

_____.

14. In that city, Neville Chamberlain, the Prime Minister of Great Britain, purchased what he called "peace in our time" by agreeing to the German occupation of part of _____.

15. Great Britain and France went to war with Germany because (Circle one.)

a. Germany marched into France   b. Germany bombed London
c. A German submarine blew up a British passenger ship   d. Germany invaded Poland   e. Germany blockaded the English Channel

16. Which of the following European countries were not occupied by Germany during World War II? (Circle one.)

    a. Norway   b. Sweden   c. France   d. The Netherlands
    e. Hungary

17. The notion of German racial superiority figured prominently in Nazi ideology; indeed, the Nazis referred to the German people as the

    _____ Race. Signs of German racial superiority included blond   hair,   blue   eyes,   and   supposed   descent   from   pure

    _____ stock.

18. The Nazi plan for the extermination of European Jewry was referred to

    as   the   _____   _____   to   the   Jewish Problem.

19. Julius Streicher edited a newspaper primarily devoted to depicting the Jew in extremely negative and grotesque terms. This newspaper was

    called _____.

20. More than 6 million Jews were murdered during the Holocaust. The largest number, more than 2 million, were from (Circle one.)

    a. Holland   b. Germany   c. Poland   d. Russia   e. Rumania

21. Which of the following was not a concentration camp? (Circle one.)

    a. Hamburg   b. Buchenwald   c. Auschwitz   d. Majdanek
    e. Treblinka   f. Bergen-Belsen

22. True or false? The Germans were aided in their crimes against the Jewish people by the active aid of local populations of countries that they occupied. T [   ]   F [   ]

23. A country that acquitted itself with particular honor during the

    Holocaust was _____. Its king and citizens threatened to put on yellow stars to express their spiritual solidarity with the Jews, and to prevent their being singled out by the Germans; and at great risk to themselves, the citizens smuggled the Jews out of their country.

24. After the Holocaust, a new term came into use that described the systematic destruction of an entire people. This term is

    _____.

TRUE OR FALSE? *

1. Most Israelis view the Holocaust as a historical fluke, a bizarre instance of a nation gone mad, which is not likely to happen again. T [   ]   F [   ]

2. Israelis are torn in their feelings about the Holocaust. At times they do everything that they can to keep the memories of that tragedy alive; at other times, they try to ignore and forget it. T [   ]   F [   ]

3. Many Israelis believe that the world at large bears a measure of moral responsibility for the Holocaust. T [   ]   F [   ]

4. Israelis feel that they, too, share a measure of responsibility for what happened. T [   ]   F [   ]

5. Many others were killed during World War II, but no group could match the Jews in numbers of people lost. T [   ]   F [   ]

6. The Holocaust was carried out by relatively few people, those who were members of the Nazi party. T [   ]   F [   ]

7. Once Germany began its systematic persecution of the Jews, the idea captured the imagination of other European governments. T [   ]   F [   ]

8. One of the reasons for the White Paper was that the British worried about the reactions of the Arab population in Palestine to Jewish immigration. T [   ]   F [   ]

9. The Arabs proved to be staunch allies in the fight against Germany during World War II. T [   ]   F [   ]

10. The British allowed Jews from the Yishuv to enlist in their armed forces because they knew how desperately the Jews wanted to fight the Germans. T [   ]   F [   ]

ISSUES IN DEPTH

Support the following general statements with specific references from the text (quotations or your summary).

1. Anti-Semitism was not a malady confined to the Germans alone during World War II.

_____

_____

2. The British often placed political factors over moral considerations on their list of priorities.

_____

_____

3. The Holocaust was but one instance of inhumanity practiced on a mass scale.

_____

_____

4. Israelis often feel that the Holocaust can be repeated in other settings and circumstances today.

_____

_____

5. Arab leaders in the past demonstrated that their hatred of Jews was not confined to those who settled in Israel, but extended to Jewry in general.

_____

_____

6. The Jews of the Yishuv desperately wanted to do something to express their solidarity with the victims of the Holocaust.

_____

_____

7. The German people showed a remarkable capacity for morally taking in stride the monstrous acts perpetrated by their government.

_____

_____

8. After the war, when the horror of the Holocaust was bared for all to see, governments and officials retained their capacity to remain blind, or insensitive, to Jewish suffering.

_____

_____

IDENTIFY THE FOLLOWING *

1. The center in Jerusalem set up as a memorial to the victims of the Holocaust _____

2. The people who suffered an experience (systematic extermination) that most closely resembles what happened to the Jews during the Holocaust _____

3. The name and position of the Arab leader who was treated to a "tour" of Jewish agony in Auschwitz

_____

4. The Jewish military unit that fought the Germans under the British flag _____

5. Name at least three European countries that showed a capacity and willingness to echo the anti-Semitic refrain of Nazi Germany

   _____

6. The document issued by the British which placed a severe limit upon Jewish immigration to Palestine

   _____

   _____

7. The military skill of those Palestinian Jews sent into occupied Europe to make contact with members of Jewish communities living under the Nazi yoke _____

8. The event in Israel in the early sixties which dramatized the horror of the Holocaust, both for younger Israelis and for the world at large

   _____

HISTORICAL MEMOS

Imagine that you were a Jewish official during and after World War II, charged with the responsibility of clarifying the problems of your people, and persuading those in positions of power to respond positively to your requests. What points would you make in memoranda to these people?

1. Edward Stettinius, the U.S. Secretary of State

2. A Palestinian Arab leader, worrying about the effects of Jewish immigration, and therefore actively supporting the White Paper

3. American Jewish communal leaders, as regards steps that they might take to help

4. Ernest Bevin, in the years between the end of World War II and the creation of Israel

5. A German friend, whom you knew before the war, who confesses his distaste for Nazism, but insists that as a loyal citizen of his country, he must go along and obey the orders of those in authority; there are two factors involved, he tells you: patriotism, and the fact that he can really do nothing to change things

6. A British official from whom you wish to obtain permission to send Jewish parachutists into occupied Europe

MEANINGS AND IMPLICATIONS

In a sentence or two, explain the meanings and/or purposes of the following excerpts from the text:

1. "Business as usual" _____

_____

2. The British general's description of Jewish refugees as "well-fed, healthy, and robust, their pockets bulging with money" _____

_____

3. "Young Israelis, especially, have come to believe that the singling out of Jews for extermination was possible only because the Jews had no country of their own. Six million perished not because they lacked courage, but because they lacked any way to put such courage into practice" _____

_____

4. "Dr. Nahum Goldmann. . .admitted that . . . 'we were too impressed. . . with the argument that the [Allied] generals should be left in peace to fight the war'" _____

_____

5. Chaim Guri's observation after the Eichmann trial that "free men will turn from time to time to look at their receding past without freezing into pillars of salt. They will be wiser. They will not evict from their souls this chapter in the chronicles of life but will live it fully, unashamed. Only then will they endow their liberty its truest meaning: that it is not self-evident"_____

_____

Chapter Nineteen

A Permanent State of Siege

EXCERPTS FROM A DIARY

The excerpts below might have been taken from the diary of a vatik, a veteran pioneer who has lived in Israel since World War I. To which event, situation, or attitude in the text does each excerpt refer?

1. If he means what he says, maybe, just maybe, we will live in peace with one another. And when you come right down to it, why shouldn't we?

    _____

    _____

2. What she is saying is that we choose life, not death.

    _____

    _____

3. Why couldn't they keep out of it? Now because of their greed, there will be bitterness and bloodshed for years to come.

    _____

    _____

4. It's unbelievable. The country changes and develops from day to day. If someone were to go away for a year or two he wouldn't recognize it. And just two years ago, we were worrying about survival.

    _____

    _____

5. He may come from the richest country in the world, but he is one very confused young man. I just don't understand all of this nonsense about "What is a Jew?" and "Why am I a Jew?" The way I see it, a person's a Jew because he is a Jew, period! And he acts accordingly!

    _____

    _____

6. Okay, she may have been a bit too blunt and forthright for American

sensibilities, but they asked for it and she told it, as it is, now, and as it will be for a long time to come.

_____

_____

7. Is this what he means by national honor and recapturing the ancient glories of the Pharaohs? Couldn't he have come up with something more constructive?

_____

_____

8. War again! Will this vicious cycle of needless destruction never end? And all because of a big lie, a trumped-up charge whose falseness is so evident to anyone who cares to check the facts!

_____

_____

9. In a way this is worse than an all-out war. You never know who or where the enemy is, when he will strike, or at whom. And more often than not, the victims are unarmed civilians, unsuspecting and defenseless. This is terror at its cruelest.

_____

_____

10. This is hardly the beginning that we had in mind. No Zionist thinker ever imagined a culmination of this sort — besieged on all sides, our very survival a gamble. I don't think we will perish; we'll hold out despite all predictions to the contrary. But the process of creation is marked by our blood, and the blood of our neighbors.

_____

_____

_____

A PEACEMAKER'S PROBLEMS

You are not expected to be a miracle worker in this activity, or to make a definitive diplomatic breakthrough. However, you might find it interesting to put your common sense to work, unraveling the assortment of snags that have kept Israel and its Arab neighbors in a persisting state of deadlock over the years. What suggestions would you make to resolve the following

Mediterranean Sea

Golan Heights

West Bank
Jerusalem

Gaza

ISRAEL

Sinai Peninsula

Administered Territories

issues in a manner that might be acceptable both to Israel and to the particular Arab government or group in question?

1. THE SINAI PENINSULA

   a. Egypt insists upon recovering the entire peninsula, and retaining the right as the sovereign authority to station troops wherever it pleases.

   b. Israel feels that there should be an adjustment of borders for reasons of national security. It further insists that it will never accept the presence of large contingents of Egyptian troops within firing range, and would like to see the entire peninsula demilitarized. Finally, inasmuch as the Straits of Tiran represent a vital sea lane to the Jewish state (and Egypt's arbitrary closing of these waters to Israeli shipping was a main cause of the Six Day War, acknowledged as such by the international community), Israel wants to maintain a military presence in Sharm el Sheikh, to insure the security of vessels traveling to and from its southern port. These waters are considered an economic lifeline to Israel and must remain open.

   _____

   _____

   _____

2. THE GOLAN HEIGHTS

   a. Syria demands the unconditional return of the Golan Heights as a prelude to any talk of settlement with Israel.

   b. The Golan Heights overlook all of northern Israel — its cities, towns, and farming settlements. Until it was seized by the Israeli army in the Six Day War, Syrian artillery could rain death and destruction upon this entire area at will. Israel, therefore, though it has not annexed the Golan Heights, and insists that everything is negotiable, would be loathe to give up the Heights, and has established a number of settlements in this area. An unconditional return of the Golan Heights to Syria would constitute an intolerable security risk to Israel, and would unquestionably provoke a political crisis in the country.

   _____

_____

_____

_____

3. JERUSALEM (the Old City)

   a. The Arabs demand that the Old City of Jerusalem be returned to Moslem rule, either under Jordan or as part of a Palestinian state.

   b. The Israelis claim that Jerusalem is a united city, part of Israel proper, and must never again be divided. Israel formally annexed Jerusalem after the Six Day War, and insists that its status is non-negotiable; however, it has always safeguarded Christian and Moslem holy places.

_____

_____

_____

_____

4. THE WEST BANK

   a. The Arab governments demand that the entire West Bank, including the Old City of Jerusalem, be converted (along with the Gaza Strip, with a connection between these two areas running through Israel) to a Palestinian state, in all likelihood under the control of the P.L.O. The "moderates" of the P.L.O. accept this arrangement as a first stage (so they feel compelled to claim, perhaps for political reasons) in the liberation of their homeland. (This is a polite way of describing the "dismantling" of Israel and establishing in its place a secular democratic state, where Jews, Christians, and Moslems will live in peace. Since the Lebanese Civil War, however, this approach has been played down and discredited.)

   b. The Israelis, though willing to give back a considerable portion of the West Bank, insist upon adjusting the borders. The pre-1967 lines jutted into Israel's highly vulnerable center. With one successful military thrust by the enemy in time of war, the country could be cut in half. Furthermore, Israel refuses to accept the idea of an armed, radicalized, sovereign Palestinian state on its borders, dedicated to its destruction. It insists that any such entity be under Jordanian authority for the foreseeable future.

_____

_____

_____

_____

MAP STUDY

The maps below represent wars, or modifications thereof, fought by Israel and its neighbors. On the basis of the lines of battle, troop alignments, and Israel's borders, match the following names with the appropriate map:

1. War of Independence
2. Sinai Campaign
3. Six Day War
4. War of Attrition 1968-70
5. Yom Kippur War
6. First Israeli-Egyptian Disengagement Agreement, January 1974
7. Israeli-Syrian Disengagement Agreement, May 1974

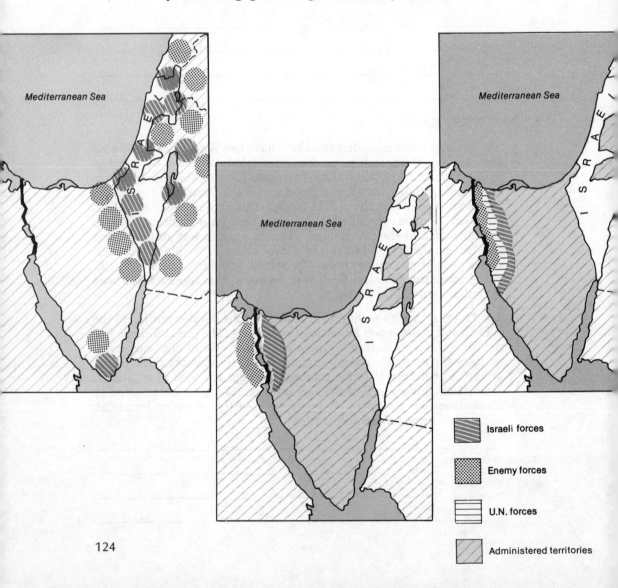

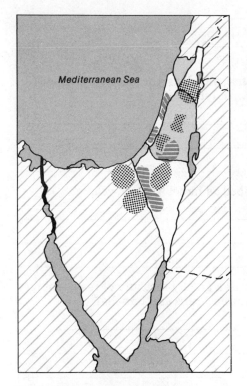

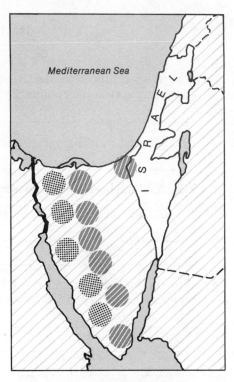

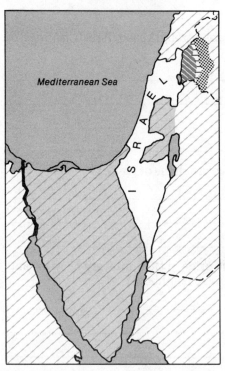

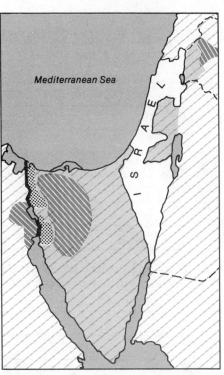

INSIGHTS

1. Why does Golda Meir declare that aliyah is the best way American Jews can express their solidarity with Israel?

   _____

   _____

   _____

2. Why has "ein brerah" been described as Israel's secret weapon?

   _____

   _____

3. Why do the British and French bear a goodly measure of responsibility for the eruption of conflict between the Arabs and Israelis?

   _____

   _____

   _____

4. Why has the conflict with the Arabs strengthened Israeli feelings of identity and responsibility?

   _____

   _____

   _____

5. Why do American Jews so often have problems of identity?

   _____

   _____

6. Why do Israelis have relatively little pride in their military prowess and harbor so little hatred toward their Arab neighbors?

   _____

   _____

FORMATIVE EXPERIENCES

People, attitudes, and issues are shaped by specific and vivid experiences. Which experiences have figured most prominently in the development of the following?

1. A 30-year-old Israeli

2. A 75-year-old Israeli

3. A 30-year-old American Jew

4. A 75-year-old American Jew

5. A 50-year-old Palestinian Arab refugee

6. The continuing Arab-Israeli conflict

7. The mentality of siege and isolation that has characterized Israeli thinking for so long

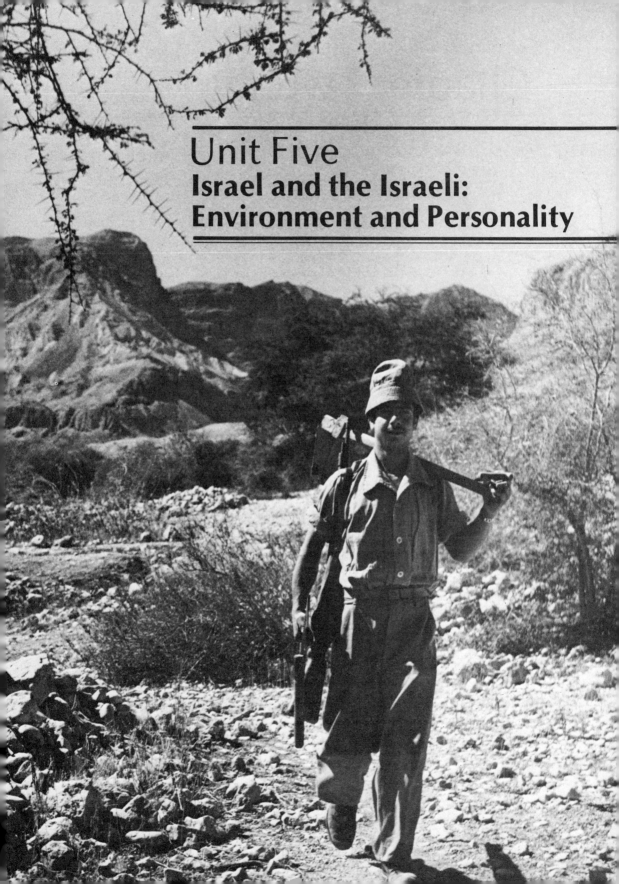

Unit Five
Israel and the Israeli:
Environment and Personality

Chapter Twenty

The "Tough" Sabra

THE SABRA IN PERSPECTIVE *

---

1. Why is the sabra called by this name, and what does it signify?

   _____

   _____

2. Which of the following is not, in all likelihood, one of the elements of the sabra's experience? (Circle one, and explain the reason for your choice.)

   a. A rapidly changing society
   b. Immigrant parents, grandparents, or relatives
   c. The constant presence of danger
   d. Some kind of military experience
   e. The frustrations of being a religious minority
   f. Differences of opinion with the older generation
   g. Confusion about the meaning and implications of Jewish identity

   _____

   _____

3. Which of the following responsibilities has the sabra probably not been called upon to fulfill in some fashion or form? (Circle and explain.)

   a. To defend the Jewish homeland
   b. To extend a helping hand to persecuted Jews outside of Israel
   c. To win acceptance in international high society
   d. To participate in the creation of a national Jewish culture
   e. To fulfill the values and dreams of the early pioneers
   f. To help absorb new immigrants into the life of the country

   _____

   _____

4. True or false, and why? Given their military prowess and proven successes in this sphere, the sabras can generally be characterized as hawks, rather than doves. T [ ]   F [ ]

   _____

5. How many areas can you point out in which the sabras are different from their parents or grandparents who immigrated to Israel?

_____

_____

_____

6. How many differences can you point out between the sabras and their American Jewish contemporaries?

_____

_____

ISSUES IN DEPTH

Support the following general statements with specific references to, or quotations from, the text.

1. The sabras have created a language and life-style of their own, rather than fashioning themselves along the lines of the ideological blueprints of their elders.

_____

_____

2. Israelis themselves are aware of their tendency, perhaps their need, to hold back and bottle up their emotions.

_____

_____

3. Israeli soldiers have mixed feelings about fighting wars.

_____

_____

4. The "toughness" of the sabra is more than likely an outer shell to conceal inner feelings.

_____

_____

5. The Arabs have waged war against the Israelis in a variety of ways.

_____

_____

6. Arab aggression against Israel has allowed itself a no-holds-barred approach.

_____

_____

7. The Arab-Israeli conflict contains the seeds of a potential superpower confrontation.

_____

_____

8. The Israelis have not yet learned to take casualties in their stride.

_____

_____

9. The Arabs are aware of the Israeli "casualty complex" and do not hesitate to play upon it.

_____

_____

10. Concern and compassion for the individual soldier and his or her family has become a duly institutionalized procedure in the Israeli army.

_____

_____

WHO SAID WHAT? *

The sabra is a much written about and talked about character. Match the following statements in the right column with the characters in the left column who might have made them.

1. An American Jewish tourist   _____   The young Israelis of today are so practical, so blunt, plainspoken, and matter-of-fact. I'm not complaining. They are brave and patriotic, but the sense of cause, of ideological fervor, is somehow missing.

2. A vatik from the Third Aliyah   _____   This will be the first generation of truly liberated Jews—first-class citizens, Hebrew speaking,

free of the mustiness of ghetto living, imbued with visions of social justice, and able to put their ideals into practice.

3. A sabra

_____ Sometimes they are hard to understand, and it's not always easy to relate to them. But they will put themselves out to help you in large ways and small. They taught me Hebrew, commanded me in the army, gave me a trade. So I have no complaints.

4. An Arab soldier

_____ They are so strange. So un-Jewish in their way. Or at least they are not like any Jew I have ever met. And I don't think that they really and truly grasp our life-style and problems.

5. Zionist theorist

_____ Look at them — miltarist, fascist aggressors, servants of the forces of colonialism that would enslave us all, part of a world-wide conspiracy!

6. An Oriental immigrant

_____ I'm not sure I know who I am, or what I am about. Everybody gives me advice, tries to prescribe my life, my values, my way of talking, my future. As for me, I try to live one day at a time, take my responsibilities as they come, and do the best I can.

CREATING A LIFE-STYLE

Imagine that you are married and the parent of a newborn infant, living in a neighborhood with a number of young Jewish couples in the same situation. You want your child to grow up with a strong, healthy sense of Jewish identity, which encompasses knowledge, tradition, commitment to other Jews, ties with Israel, and pride and joy in the fact of being Jewish. There are no foreseeable crises on the horizon to help you along in this process; you have to do it yourself. How would you, individually and together with your neighbors, go about creating such an environment?

AGES AND EVENTS *

This is an attempt to focus more sharply upon the swiftly moving developments and events in modern Israeli history. Below is a list of some of the more dramatic chapters in the evolution of the Jewish state (which took place before, during, and after its creation). Immediately following this list are five sabras, each born in a different time. After the year of birth, put down the developments or events in which the particular sabra was most likely to have played a role as a young adult between the ages of 18 and 35.

    a. Smuggling Holocaust victims into Israel

    b. Joining the Jewish Brigade

    c. The Yom Kippur War

    d. Working with Oriental immigrants

    e. Grasping the meaning of the Holocaust during the Eichmann trial

    f. The War of Independence

g. The Six-Day War

h. The Sinai Campaign

i. Working with immigrants from the Soviet Union

j. Parachuting into occupied Europe

k. Establishing a settlement in the Golan Heights

l. Working as shliḥim (emissaries) to teach Jewish youth from abroad the meaning and significance of the newly created Jewish state

m. Part of the first generation of children on Israel's first kibbutz

1. Born in 1915 _____

   _____

2. Born in 1925 _____

   _____

3. Born in 1935 _____

   _____

4. Born in 1945 _____

   _____

5. Born in 1955 _____

   _____

AN ISRAELI DESK DIARY

The items below could have come from the desk diary of an Israeli student. What clues do they offer as to how a sabra's Jewish identity is defined and reinforced? (Write one sentence for each item.)

1. *Friday, 2:00 P.M.*   Flowers and wine for Shabbat

   _____

2. *Sunday-Thursday*   Study the writings of the Later Prophets or the b'ḥinot bagrut (comprehensive examinations, encompassing the entire Israeli high school curriculum)

   _____

3. *Friday*   Take American cousins to Meah Shearim, the Old City of Jerusalem, and the Western Wall; later, Yad Vashem; Shabbat preparations

   _____

4. *Saturday night* Work with Avraham, Rivkah, and Moshe on costumes and decorations for Adloyada (mammoth Purim parade, celebrated on a nationwide scale)

5. *Monday* Watch preliminaries for Ḥidon HaTanach (the National Bible Quiz) on TV

6. *Tuesday* Pack for Negev tiyul (tour); brush up on archaeological data; don't forget Tanach, history books, maps of ancient Israel and special shoes for Masada climb

7. *Sunday* Begin walking at least two miles a day to get in shape for the Ts'adah (the annual four-day march to Jerusalem before Passover)

WORD SCRAMBLE *

Unscramble the following words, each of which has played a role of some kind in the unfolding experience of the sabra. Then unscramble the circled letters to make two words that describe one of the ways in which young Israelis respond to the particular circumstances of their lives. (Numbers 1–4 contain the first word; numbers 5–8, the second word.)

1. **thraed**

2. **whereb**

3. **libeb**

4. **dlan**

5. **mimatring**

6. **rutosit**

7. **labett**

8. **sintone**

Chapter Twenty-One

A Shared Experience

ISRAEL'S NATIONAL PURPOSE

The text stresses the importance of a sense of shared purpose in Israel. What does this mean?

1. In a paragraph, set down what you think Israel's national purpose should be today.

2. In the order of their importance to you, list three to five overriding priorities of the Jewish state in the final quarter of the twentieth century.

3. Can you think of any values that Israel should try to express and implement precisely because of its Jewish character?

   _____

   _____

   _____

4. Which elements of Israel's national purpose are expressed by the following activities? (Sometimes more than one element comes into play

in a single activity. And sometimes two or more activities encompass the same aims and values.)

a. Building an immigrant town

_____

b. Establishing a kibbutz

_____

c. Settling an unpopulated area in the desert, or on one of Israel's borders

_____

d. Teaching the Bible and Jewish history in the Israeli public school system

_____

e. Investing much time, money, energy, and emotion in the creation of Yad Vashem

_____

f. Serving in the Israel Defense Forces

_____

g. Creating the Law of Return, which automatically grants Israeli citizenship to any Jew who desires it

_____

h. Sending shlihim (emissaries) to Jewish communities in the Diaspora for reasons ranging from rescue and relief to education

_____

i. Observing various Jewish holidays and traditions on a nationwide scale

_____

AMERICAN JEWISH PURPOSES

1. What do you think should be the purpose, priorities and underlying values of your own Jewish community today?

_____

_____

_____

2. Which elements of Jewish communal purpose are expressed in the following activities?

   a. Belonging to synagogue or temple organizations

   _____

   b. Attending a school for Jewish studies (afternoon or day school)

   _____

   c. Visiting Israel

   _____

   d. Supporting Israel economically and politically

   _____

   e. Doing interfaith work

   _____

   f. Participating in social welfare activities within the community at large

   _____

   g. Observing various Jewish laws and traditions

   _____

   h. Encouraging a Jewish home environment

   _____

   i. Working in behalf of oppressed Jewish communities in other countries

   _____

   j. Helping disadvantaged Jews (the poor, the sick, the elderly, recently arrived immigrants) in your own community

   _____

3. If a limit were arbitrarily set upon the number of Jewish activities in which you could be involved, which three of the above would you choose, and in what order of importance? After you have made your choices, explain the reason(s) for your priorities.

VALUES AND THEIR PROBLEMS *

A society sometimes has problems precisely because of its efforts to live up to cherished values. The span of time and experience between the dream and its fulfillment is almost inevitably marked by tension, trial and error, human failings, and frustrations. This does not make the aims in question any the less urgent or authentic; it simply illuminates the thorny process involved in putting them to work. Match the statements of Jewish and Zionist values in the left column with their problematic offshoots listed in the right column.

1. The Jewish people must have a national homeland

    _____ A generation gap (defined by experience rather than chronology) between the native-born Israeli and immigrant parents and grandparents

2. Israel must open its doors and its resources to oppressed Jews everywhere

    _____ The conflicts that have divided religious and nonreligious Israelis over the years

3. A Jewish state must retain its Jewish character, and serve as a framework in which Jews of every ideological and religious persuasion may live and feel comfortable

    _____ Problems of military security, hostile neighbors, the unending threat of destruction

4. Israel must be a spiritual and cultural center for world Jewry

    _____ A social, economic, and cultural distance between Oriental and Western Jews that has been marked by tensions and resentments, as well as by progress and tangible achievements

5. The native-born Israeli will be a new Jew reared in freedom, a first-class citizen with identity and cultural roots intact, and without the external dangers, the internal insecurities and the persisting uncertainty that have haunted the Diaspora Jew

    _____ The mutual confusion as to role, responsibility, and nature of involvement that has often characterized the relations between Israelis and Diaspora Jewry

ISSUES IN DEPTH

This is a reversal of previous activities of this kind. Rather than supporting a general statement with a specific reference, in this instance the excerpt itself is the point of departure from which you formulate a general statement. What meaning or significance can be drawn from the following excerpts?

1. "When the broadcast was over—I went up to one of the men and asked if he could tell me what had happened. He. . . said. . . 'It's OK. Everyone returned safely.' And with that, having told me what was important, he walked away. Not a word about the action itself. Just 'Everyone returned safely.' " (page 157)

    _____

    _____

2. "The 'culture hero' of the Eastern European Jewish community was not a man of great physical prowess or the person who made the most money, but the scholar—the individual who proved himself able to comprehend the Talmud in its various meanings and applications." (pages 158–159)

    _____

    _____

3. "If an Arab delegate were to make a motion in the [UN] General Assembly that the world was flat, that motion would automatically receive a two-thirds majority vote." (page 158)

    _____

    _____

4. "And finally there is Abba Eban's classic remark directly after the Six Day War, in the face of Russian and Arab demands for immediate Israeli withdrawal from captured territory. For the first time in the history of human warfare, he noted, 'the victor sues for peace while the vanquished demands unconditional surrender.' " (page 158)

    _____

    _____

5. "Much of the literature . . . written . . . has as a main theme . . . war, which has been the central experience in the life of the younger generation. Not a single novel, poem, or play praises the so-called glory of war. Victories are portrayed as terrible defeats." (page 154)

    _____

    _____

6. "Because Israel is so small and its manners so informal, it is easier than it would be in bigger or older countries to know 'practically everybody,' from the prime minister to the latest soccer hero." (page 152)

_____

_____

7. "In a country as small as Israel, even 'limited' casualties are mourned by the entire nation. No one is spared the tragedy of a fallen or wounded soldier." (page 152)

_____

_____

NEWS BULLETINS AND COMMENTARIES

Israelis, being the addicted radio listeners that they are, have undoubtedly heard hundreds and even thousands of news bulletins, commentaries, and special programs over the years. See if you can figure out what the following excerpts from the airwaves refer to. All of the focal points in question are contained in this chapter.

1. From a debate: "The law of the Torah must be the law of the land; that is the meaning of a Jewish state."

_____

_____

2. From a satire: "Israel has just been censured for an act of 'defensive aggression' because it learned of a terrorist time bomb planted in Tel Aviv's central bus station, and managed to defuse it before it went off. The delegates have voted that Israel pay the P.L.O. $10,000 for the damaged explosives, and $1 million compensation for frustation and injured pride."

_____

3. From a commercial: "The people who have been hailed as the halutzim of the cosmetics industry have just achieved a dramatic breakthrough in men's cologne."

_____

_____

4. Direct news coverage: "Dignitaries from all over the country are gathered here today for the ground-breaking ceremonies. The desert heat is punishing, but they don't seem to mind at all. As one official put it, 'This is what the Zionist dream is all about, making the desert bloom

with flourishing cities that will be populated by ingathered Jews from all over the world.' "

---

5. From a news bulletin: "The whole village is in mourning."

---

6. An interview with a neighborhood leader from one of Jerusalem's poorer sections: "The way things are shaping up, there are the haves and the have-nots, and you can usually distinguish the members of each group by skin complexion."

NOT VERY LIKELY

Which of the following statements would you not be very likely to hear in an Israeli village, and why?

1. He's listening to the evening news. He'll call you back.

2. The religious parties wield a lot of political influence in the government.

3. Our daughter has volunteered to be teacher in an immigrant town that is surrounded by nothing but desert for miles around.

4. I think that pioneering can, and should, have many different meanings to many people. Why can't one be a pioneer in medicine? Or industry? Or education? Or in a variety of fields?

5. Do you know Mrs. Ya'ari, four houses down from where we live? Well, I just heard that her only son was killed in a border skirmish three months ago.

6. The UN General Assembly is meeting again. I wonder how they'll sell us out this time?

Chapter Twenty-Two

From One Generation to the Next

WHO SAID WHAT? *

On the basis of what you know about Grandfather Israel and his sabra off-spring, figure out which of the two might have made each of the statements below, at one time or another. Signify your choice by placing a G or an S in the brackets, and on the lines that follow, briefly explain why.

1. My God! It's the same story all over again: the Crusaders, the Kishinev Pogroms, the Holocaust, and now Nasser with his vow to destroy Israel. Will hatred of the Jew never cease? Will we always be a persecuted minority? [   ]

    _____

    _____

2. Why is there so little political awareness? So painful an absence of ideological commitment? An individual—indeed, society—has to think big, has to dare to dream in terms that go beyond the needs of today, to the visions of a nobler tomorrow! [   ]

    _____

    _____

3. I know it's not a nice thing to say, but I sometimes think I have more in common with the Gentiles in the United States than I do with American Jews. [   ]

    _____

    _____

4. What we need is perspective. Israel has a 4000-year history that is as wide and complicated as it is long. The creation of the Jewish state represents the latest chapter of this history — perhaps one of its most glorious and hopeful chapters, but nevertheless part of a larger process. [   ]

    _____

    _____

5. I've read about the Holocaust, thought about it, discussed it, but I must admit, the Eichmann trial was a shocker to me, a definitive turning point in my life. [   ]

_____

_____

6. Enough of all of this intellectual agonizing over the meaning of our identity and the nature of our commitment. We are a nation, plain and simple citizens of a state to whose well-being and security we must dedicate ourselves at all times and at all costs. In that sense, we are like every other state, every other people. And we have enough immediate problems on our hands without worrying about philosophy. [   ]

_____

_____

7. Yes, I guess you can say that Israel has grown by leaps and bounds. Take a look at Tel Aviv, a bustling modern metropolis with its factories and automobiles and theaters and coffee houses and throngs of people crowding the street, and it is hard to believe that this was nothing more than a stretch of sand dune a few brief decades ago. And yet, all of this progress makes me uneasy. People are becoming too materialistic, too career-minded, too comfortable. What is needed is a challenge, and the kind of discipline that comes from struggle and austerity. [   ]

_____

_____

8. During those terrible weeks before the Six Day War, I gained a new understanding of words like "ghetto," "persecution," and "pogrom." And I came to realize that in the eyes of the world, we are not Israelis, but Jews. [   ]

_____

_____

WORDS AND ATTITUDES *

The Hebrew words in this chapter are all connected in one way or another to a particular attitude. Match each Hebrew term in the left column with its related attitude in the right column.

1. Keffiye   _____ There is a time for great visions and dreams, and a time for quiet consolidation.

2. C'na'anut

_____ I don't know, maybe it's my imagination, but the young people of today seem to be lacking something—call it a spark, a sense of excitement, or idealistic passion, but there is a missing ingredient in their makeup.

3. Mah yehiyeh hasof?

_____ A profound longing to cease being different and set apart, a desire to be like other peoples.

4. Dor Bitzua

_____ A fear of the unknown that causes one to view things in the worst possible light.

5. Dor Espresso

_____ A sense of weariness that is touched, at times, with despair.

THE OTHER SIDE OF THE COIN

The distance between dream and reality is often marked by a series of puzzles, surprises, and contradictions. The sabras were part of the Zionist blueprint long before they came into being; however, like any successful creation, they took on a life of their own whose dimensions were shaped and given substance by the nature of their particular experience, rather than according to any plan. And at times, they troubled their designers, not because they digressed from the prescribed path, but precisely because they fulfilled some of Zionism's deepest expectations. Life is complicated; many of its developments have two or more sides that at times seem to stand in direct opposition to one another.

Below are a number of observations about the sabra. Some are considered positive; others negative or problematic. In the spaces following each observation, see if you can come up with alternative suggestions.

1. The sabras are the first Jews in 2000 years who have not been members of a minority. On the other hand,

2. The sabra has often been accused of being too practical, too occupied with the problems of the here and now, and too little concerned with questions of ideology. On the other hand,

3. The sabra has never experienced anti-Semitism, has never suffered a pogrom, has never known the gnaw of uncertainty that has haunted the Diaspora Jew. On the other hand,

4. The sabra has been criticized for taking a long leap backward into the biblical past and identifying with it to the exclusion of 2000 years of Diaspora history. On the other hand,

5. The sabra has always lived with tension and danger, punctuated by out-breaks of full-scale war. On the other hand,

POLITICS AND POETRY *

Poetry is, among other things, the effort to express thought and feelings through crystallized, carefully crafted verbal images. At times a line of poetry can evoke a rich world of meaning. Political speeches, on the other hand, are usually associated with length, expansiveness, and a notable absence of verbal economy and precision. And yet, at their best, these two forms of communication can express similar ideas and values. Each of the statements below is an imaginary excerpt from a political speech. Find the sentence or phrase from the Israeli songs represented in "An Army that Sings" (Related Themes, page 163) that makes the same point poetically.

1. We look forward to the day when we can afford to make significant cuts

in defense spending and can convert military equipment to civilian uses. This will give a much-needed boost to our economic productivity.

2. I firmly believe that tensions will lessen and prospects for a negotiated settlement will improve considerably in the foreseeable future. However, we must be patient.

3. It's hard to believe that right here on the ground where this shopping center now stands, dedicated young men and women fought and died in defense of our country. And it is in their name, and in honor of their sacrifices, that I proudly call this street "Independence Square."

INSIGHTS

1. Why are younger Israelis less baffled and frightened by the Arabs, and more able to see their point of view, than are their elders?

2. Why were the vatikim troubled by the normalization of Israeli youth, a goal that they themselves had always dreamed of and worked toward?

3. Why did C'na'anut come into vogue among Israeli youth during the first years of statehood?

THE ISRAELI GENERATION GAP

While no one denies that there are distances of outlook, experience, and culture that separate Grandfather Israel from his native-born children, there are also a number of powerful factors and forces that draw them together.

1. What are the elements that divide the generations?

2. What are the elements that unite them?

Chapter Twenty-Three

Israel and the Arab Refugees

ASPECTS OF THE REFUGEE SITUATION *

1. (Circle the correct answer.) The plight of the Palestinian refugees became a particularly pressing issue of conscience for many Israelis

   a. With the appearance of Amos Oz's novel, *My Michael*   b. With the coming to prominence of the P.L.O., whose terrorist tactics dramatized the desperation of the Palestinians   c. With the creation of the policy that allowed Arabs from other countries to visit relatives in occupied territories and in Israel proper, thus bringing about a measure of face-to-face contact and personal dialogue between the Israelis and their neighbors   d. Directly after the Six Day War in 1967   e. With the arrival of hundreds of thousands of Jewish refugees from various Arab countries, from 1947 until 1963

2. Which of the following was *not* a factor in precipitating the Israeli crisis of conscience with regard to the Palestinian refugees? (Circle the correct answer.)

   a. A firsthand view of the refugee camps   b. The sober realization that the Palestinians were the crux of the Middle East conflict, and that if their problem were not solved there could be no negotiated settlement with the various Arab governments   c. Underlying feelings of guilt   d. Associations with the Holocaust   e. A sense of identification with a people who have been called the Jews of the Middle East, rootless exiles and refugees

   In the lines below, explain the reason for your choice.

   _____

   _____

   _____

3. Israel's decision to allow Arabs living in the areas it captured during the Six Day War to travel freely to Jordan (and through Jordan to other

   Arab countries) is called the _____ _____ policy.

4. True or false, and why? The policy of allowing Arabs in Israel proper and in the occupied areas to travel freely has, except for the period

150

directly after the Yom Kippur War, persisted without interruption until this very day. T [ ] F [ ]

_____

_____

5. True or false, and why? Israel has constantly demonstrated its willingness to tackle the refugee problem in concrete terms. T [ ] F [ ]

_____

_____

ISSUES IN DEPTH

Support the following general statements with specific quotations from, or references to, the text:

1. It has been observed that at times Israelis are not only aware of their history; they are haunted by it.

_____

_____

_____

2. A child growing up in the refugee camps before 1967 was explicitly taught to hate the Israelis.

_____

_____

_____

3. An Israeli might well claim that on the question of refugees a double standard is applied to Israel and the Arab governments.

_____

_____

_____

4. From the moment of its creation, Israel has forthrightly acknowledged the rights of its Arab inhabitants.

_____

_____

_____

5. The policies and attitudes of the various Arab governments have played a major role in the continuing plight of the refugees.

_____

_____

_____

6. Israelis, particularly the younger generation, have shown an awareness of, and sensitivity to, the moral implications of the refugee problem.

_____

_____

_____

SECURITY RISK

Imagine that you are a young Israeli watching over the flow of Arab traffic to and from Israel, in accordance with the Open-Bridges policy. A tourist approaches you, wants to know why this is permitted. After all, isn't it a large risk, clearly endangering both Israeli lives and national security, opening the door to spies and terrorists? How would you explain the reasons — political, psychological, and moral — for this admittedly risky program?

HISTORY'S HEADLINES *

Which events, issues, and/or general developments related to the refugee problem do the following headlines suggest?

1. ARAB STATUS IN ISRAEL GUARANTEED; DOWN IN BLACK AND WHITE!

2. ISRAEL'S POPULATION EXPLOSION REACHES A NEW HIGH — 100%; NO END IN SIGHT!

3. LATEST OFFER REBUFFED! COMPROMISE OUT OF THE QUESTION, ARAB LEADERS DECLARE.

4. TEARFUL REUNION. BROTHER AND SISTER SEPARATED BY WAR MEET FOR FIRST TIME SINCE 1948.

5. BOOK PORTRAYS TROUBLED VICTORS GRAPPLING WITH TOUGH MORAL QUESTION.

EDITORIALS *

In a related vein, to which issues and events are the following editorial excerpts addressed?

1. Their concern for the displaced is truly touching, but what they offer is tokens, crumbs. A payment here, a conference there, allowing a small percentage to return to their rightful homes — but that is not the heart of the problem. And until justice is done, there can be no talk of peace!

---

2. Some people are making this an issue of academic freedom. They say that these are their children, to educate as they wish. However, there is a difference between liberty and license. Using the privilege of academic freedom to lie, to distort, to inspire hatred, is to violate the essence of everything we talk about. And that these lies are, in effect, supported by the international community is outrageous.

---

3. Ideology and lofty values are fine, but in themselves are not enough to cope with the overwhelming challenge before us. We must be tough, resourceful, practical, and patient. We must build houses, create jobs,

set up language programs, establish new communities. And above all, we must guard against the social and cultural tensions that are almost inevitable in a situation of this sort. We are, in fact, being asked to perform a major miracle, and have no choice but to rise to the occasion.

4. Maybe it will work; maybe it won't. If it does, it is a major breakthrough, regardless of whatever else happens. And who knows, maybe this is the way to real peace — people from both sides coming into daily contact, learning to know one another, building mutual trust. It is a long shot. And it is dangerous. But we've got to try!

INSIGHTS

1. Why do Israelis feel "both sympathy and hostility toward the Arabs"?

2. Why is an "emotional détente—a precondition for any peace settlement" in the Middle East?

3. Why are the 650,000 Jewish refugees from Arab lands not considered a problem in the sense that the Palestinian refugees are?

4. Why have Arab governments consistently refused to try to solve the refugee problem over the years?

5. Why is it "easier to *feel* the Palestinians' tragedy than it is to find a solution for it that would not only be acceptable to them but would also prevent an even greater tragedy for Jews"?

_____

_____

_____

SIMILARITIES AND DIFFERENCES

The Middle East conflict has, indeed, created two groups of refugees — Jews and Arabs. In the spaces below, fill in as many similarities and differences between the two groups as you can. (Compare notes with your classmates.)

1. Similarities include_____

_____

_____

2. Differences include

Jews	Arabs
a. _____	_____
_____	_____
b. _____	_____
_____	_____
c. _____	_____
_____	_____
d. _____	_____
_____	_____
e. _____	_____
_____	_____
_____	_____
_____	_____
_____	_____

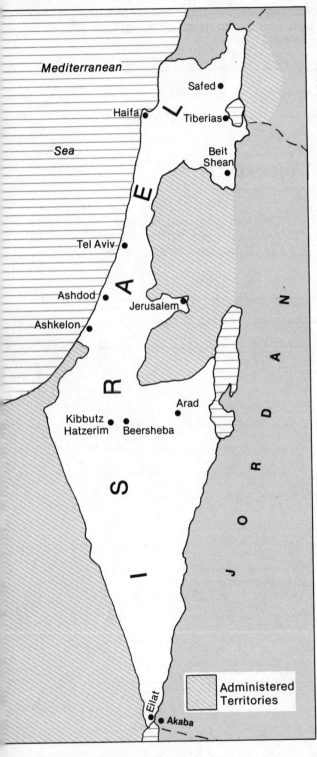

Mediterranean

Safed ●

Haifa ●   Tiberias ●

Sea

Beit
Shean ●

Tel Aviv ●

Ashdod ●
        Jerusalem ●

Ashkelon ●

Arad ●

Kibbutz ● ●
Hatzerim Beersheba

Eilat
● Akaba

Administered
Territories

AN ARAB TOUR OF ISRAEL *

Since the early 1970's, Arabs from
neighboring lands have been able to
visit their relatives in Israel, and to
move freely within the country for the
duration of their stay. What is it like
to see Israel through Arab eyes? How
would an Israeli Arab explain some
of the sights of the Jewish state to his
or her relatives from abroad, without
reference either to Zionist theory or
Jewish history? Below is a map
featuring some of Israel's more
famous landmarks. The statements
following the map could, conceivably,
be the way an Israeli Arab might talk
about that landmark. In the spaces
after each description, fill in the
location (from the map) that you
think is being referred to.

1. This is a seaside town that is
    fairly bursting with treasures
    from the past, an archaeological
    paradise with remnants of
    many civilizations. At one time,
    this was a famous center of the

    ancient Philistines. _____

    _____

2. This is a special kind of com-
    munity. People don't receive
    salaries for their labor. They are
    paid, instead, with food, shelter,
    goods and services. The women
    are thoroughly emancipated and
    enjoy equal status with the men.
    The children live in special
    houses. And something strange
    — one of the members here is
    also   a   member   of   the
    Parliament, and when he comes
    home for a day, he is put to work

    in the kitchen. _____

    _____

3. This is a major port city, and it has a sizable number of Arab residents. It extends from the top of the mountain right on down to the shore line. And the view from the top is positively breathtaking.

_____

4. This city is a stone's throw from the famous Jordanian city where the king often vacations. And farther out, you can see the Saudi Arabian shoreline. _____

_____

5. This is the site of a seaport more than 4000 years old.

_____

6. Twenty years ago, this city was reminiscent of a frontier town in the American Wild West. Now, of course, everything has changed, and it is as modern and civilized as any other metropolis.

_____

7. This used to be the no-man's-land that separated the New City from the Old City. You'll feel right at home in the market place you're about to see. _____

_____

8. Don't get confused by the faces, or by the Arabic language. These people are Jews. This is what is called an immigrant town.

_____

VALUE ANALYSIS

What values are expressed by the following? (At times, the same value may come into play on several occasions; at other times, two or more values may relate to one occasion.)

1. Israel's promise, duly set down in its Declaration of Independence, to its Arab inhabitants "of full and equal citizenship and due representation"

_____

_____

2. The Open-Bridges policy

_____

_____

3. The persisting refusal of various Arab governments to negotiate a solution of the refugee problem with Israel

_____

_____

4. Israeli guilt over the problem of the Palestinian refugees

_____

_____

5. Israel's absorption of some 650,000 Jewish refugees from Arab countries

_____

_____

6. Arab propaganda regarding Israel

_____

_____

Unit Six
The Israeli Way of Life

Chapter Twenty-Four

Archaeology and the National Consciousness

A SEARCH FOR UNDERSTANDING *

Fill in the blank spaces below with the appropriate word or words.

1. In Israel, archaeology is so popular a pastime that it has been compared to baseball or football in this country, in the sense of its being

    _____ _____; indeed, the Israeli passion for digging into the ancient past has been described as a

    _____, or a consuming hunger; an urgent, insatiable drive.

2. Among the reasons given for this preoccupation with the past is the

    Israeli need for visible proof of Jewish_____ in Eretz Israel which extends back to biblical times. Given the chopped up nature of Jewish history in the Diaspora, Israelis look to ancient relics and ruins

    to help establish lines of_____ between then and now. This need has become particularly pressing in the face of

    _____ claims that the Israelis are intruders who have no place in the Middle East and no legitimate right to the land.

3. If a person were about to begin an archaeological tour through Israel, he

    or she would be wise to include the _____ on a list of "must" items to be taken along, for it can serve as a singularly valuable guidebook and source of reference. That Israelis are well aware of this unique historical key, and pride themselves in their knowledge of its

    contents, is attested by the _____ _____

    _____, a yearly event that commands nationwide interest.

4. This "guide book" contains two major ideals of the Zionist pioneers, which continue to be central aims of the modern Jewish state. These

    ideals are _____ _____ and _____

    _____ _____ _____.

5. Such discoveries as _____, a monument to Jewish determination to live in freedom at all costs; the _____ _____ _____, which have been regarded by many Israelis as written evidence of their right to the land; and the accidental unearthing of an ancient _____ on the grounds of one of the early kibbutzim, make the countless hours of patient digging worthwhile for most Israelis, and are the logical reasons why archaeology will probably retain its hold on, and cherished place in, the national imagination.

SPEECHES OF SIGNIFICANCE *

Archaeology, being the national pastime that it is in the Jewish state, has moved many an Israeli public figure to deliver a speech on the occasion of a new and potentially significant discovery. Match the possible excerpts from public speeches in the right column with the places, events, and states of mind that they refer to in the left column.

1. The Western Wall of the ____ Second Temple in the Old City of Jerusalem

These relics, dusty and crumbling with age, record the close ties between our tradition then and now, and strengthen our resolve to create a Third Commonwealth in the difficult weeks and months ahead.

2. The discovery of Hebrew-____ Arab peasants in Pekiin

Let me assure the world at large that we are not insane; we are fully aware of the destructive capacities of advanced weapons, and of the consequences that would ensue from unleashing them

3. A ceremony on Masada

____ We have gathered here not only to celebrate scholarship or to applaud knowledge, but to affirm the ties, the deep and persisting involvement, between our people and their ancient tradition

4. Discovery of the Dead Sea ____ All of this gloomy
    Scrolls   speculation leaves most
                                 Israelis cold. Death wishes
                                 are emphatically *not* a part
                                 of our national psychology.
                                 We have come to this coun-
                                 try to create, to build a life
                                 for ourselves and our
                                 children; to nurture and
                                 nourish hope, not to perish
                                 in glory

5. Opening the annual Ḥidon ____ The volunteers who have
    HaTanach   made this discovery
                                 possible prove that the
                                 Jewish people are one
                                 people with a shared
                                 history, culture, and com-
                                 mitment, regardless of the
                                 respective ideologies that
                                 they happen to embrace.

6. The Masada Complex   ____ The excavations of this
                                 site, which were begun, of
                                 course, only after June
                                 1967, have yielded a num-
                                 ber of finds that confirm
                                 the accuracy of ancient ac-
                                 counts.

7. Discovery of a sixth-century ____ Here is living proof that
    synagogue at Bet Alpha   there has been a con-
                                 tinuous Jewish presence in
                                 the land of Israel from an-
                                 cient times until today.

8. The Samson complex   ____ Everything here, every-
                                 thing that you see before
                                 you, is scarred and sacred
                                 testimony that the values
                                 proclaimed at the Exodus
                                 from Egypt, and reaf-
                                 firmed when the Zionist
                                 pioneers rejected the coils
                                 of a crippled Jewish life in
                                 the Diaspora, have been
                                 alive in one form or another
                                 throughout Jewish history.

MEANINGS AND IMPLICATIONS

Briefly explain the meanings of each of the quotations below.

1. "More than the Jewish people preserved the Sabbath, the Sabbath preserved the Jewish people."

_____

_____

_____

2. "Through archaeology they discover their 'religious values.' In archaeology they find their religion. They learn that their forefathers were in this country 3000 years ago. This is a value."

_____

_____

_____

3. "For Israelis, the [Dead Sea] scrolls have since assumed an almost sacred quality. In the eyes of some, the scrolls are like titles of real estate, like deeds of possession to a contested country."

_____

_____

_____

4. "In the 1930's, when the Jews of Germany were becoming ever more isolated and anxious about their situation, there was a dramatic demand for Jewish encyclopedias and books of Jewish history and Hebrew grammar."

_____

_____

_____

5. "This title [Herzl's _Altneuland,_ "The Old-New Land"] captures the view that most Israelis have of their country and of themselves. What they do — building, reclaiming land... — is aimed at the future. But their sense of who they are and where they are going is rooted in Israel's ancient past."

_____

_____

_____

TRUE OR FALSE? *

1. The Dead Sea Scrolls strengthened the belief of Israelis in their long-standing connection with, and right to, the land in which they lived.
T [ ] F [ ]

2. A bulmus is a seal that is placed upon every major archaeological discovery. T [ ] F [ ]

3. Israel's alleged "Masada complex" worries outside observers who feel that if the Jewish state were in danger of being destroyed, it would unleash nuclear weapons, which could trigger a world war. T [ ] F [ ]

4. During the 1930's, many German Jews responded to their increasingly difficult situation by turning to Jewish culture and tradition.
T [ ] F [ ]

5. Herzl's novel ("The Old-New Land") attested to his interest in, and commitment to, the ancient Jewish past. T [ ] F [ ]

6. Arab opposition to the existence of Israel over the years has been one of the factors that have moved the Israelis to make archaeology their "national sport." T [ ] F [ ]

7. The early pioneers were largely uninterested in archaeology because they were determined to cut ties with the past and concentrate solely upon the future. T [ ] F [ ]

8. One of the reasons why the Hidon HaTanach commands so much interest is that most Israelis know the Bible and cherish it. T [ ] F [ ]

ISRAELIS AND THE BIBLE

Imagine that you are an Israeli with an American Jewish pen pal, who has heard about the special relationship between Israelis and the Bible, and would like to know your thoughts on the subject. What does the Bible mean to you? What role has it played in your life, and in the life of the nation at large? In a paragraph, how would you sum up the place and significance of the Bible in Israel today?

In a second paragraph, set down what you think are the major differences between the role of the Bible in Israel and in the Diaspora.

AN ARCHAEOLOGICAL BIBLE QUIZ *

Archaeologists are historical detectives in their way. A ruin here, a piece of pottery there, a drawing on the wall — and lo and behold, they begin to reconstruct the story of an ancient civilization. Granted, it is not that simple: years of training, countless hours of research, painstaking work, patience, and a healthy measure of faith all go into the process of discovery. Still, they are able to deduce so much from (relatively) so little. The following groups of imaginary "finds" could have been unearthed at the sites of several imaginary archaeological excavations. Try to figure out to which biblical event each of these groups refer. The answers to this quiz can be found on page 218.

1. A broken sign that says, *"STRAW HUTS FOR SALE."* A remnant of papyrus, with the headline " 'SWIMMING LESSONS TO BE PART OF MILITARY TRAINING FROM NOW ON!' EGYPTIAN GENERAL DECLARES." And on the same piece of papyrus, further down, a smaller headline reads. "LABOR MARKET IN STATE OF UPHEAVAL!"

2. On top of Mount Moriah, an ancient altar has been discovered. At its side is a rope that has been cut in a number of places, and a little farther away are pieces of an object that when put together resemble a shofar.

3. A number of broken signs clumped together in an ancient building that was once a center for public gatherings. The slogans on the signs read; *"SEPARATE RELIGION AND STATE!" "KINGDOM NOW!"* and *"EVERYONE'S DOING IT—WHY NOT US!"*

4. A table with Hebrew writing on it, broken into little pieces, next to a hoof and a narrow tail made out of gold.

5. A 4000-year-old diary that reads, "I just returned from the celebration. Everyone was there toasting the happy parents. This blessed event has got to go down in history as a medical miracle — a triumph of faith over fact."

Chapter Twenty-Five

The Political Style

INSIGHTS

1. Why are Israelis essentially skeptical about political authority?

   _____

   _____

   _____

2. Why do religious groups in Israel manage to wield so much political power?

   _____

   _____

   _____

3. Why has the issue of religion in Israel become so bitter and divisive a problem?

   _____

   _____

   _____

4. Why has there been no emergence of a military ruling class, despite the fact that Israel's continuing state of siege offers a singularly favorable setting for such a development?

   _____

   _____

   _____

5. Why has no political party, including that headed by Ben-Gurion at the height of his prestige, ever managed to achieve a clear majority (51 percent or more of the popular vote) in an Israeli election?

   _____

   _____

6. Why have there always been so many political parties in Israel?

_____

_____

FORMS OF GOVERNMENT *

The statements below can be applied to either an American-style democracy (with the president as the head of both state and government, elections along personal rather than party lines, etc.), a parliamentary democracy such as that which exists in Israel, or a totalitarian government. Identify the form of government suggested by each statement. Let *A* stand for an American-style democracy, *P* for a parliamentary democracy, and *T* for a totalitarian government. In the spaces underneath, briefly explain the reasons for your choice.

1. He has the best chance to be elected because he comes over so impressively on television. [   ]

_____

_____

2. Who knows the reasons for this policy? We simply have to assume that the government has our best interests at heart. [   ]

_____

_____

3. No one knows what happened. He was accused of committing crimes against the state, and has never been heard from since. [   ]

_____

_____

4. This last vote of no confidence has brought down the government. The president is conferring with the leaders of every major party to see who will form the next government. [   ]

_____

_____

5. That kind of foreign policy decision must be left in the hands of the president. The legislative bodies can only ratify or not ratify his actions, as the case may be; they cannot initiate foreign policy. [   ]

_____

_____

6. General X has been the head of government and state for six years, but he has promised to return to civilian rule as soon as internal conditions stabilize, and the economy makes a significant recovery. [   ]

_____

_____

7. One of the biggest problems challenging our political system today is that people are voting more and more on the basis of personality and less and less on the basis of interests or issues. [   ]

_____

_____

8. The individual is a cog in the wheel of national progress. His rights and interests are only important insofar as they do not interfere with the well-being, or authority, of the state. [   ]

_____

_____

9. Her election is practically assured. She is number 12 on her party list, and every poll in the country has that party leading by a ratio of two to one. [   ]

_____

_____

10. The best way to choose a national leader is to hold a televised debate, in order to see where the two candidates stand on the issues, and how they handle themselves under pressure. [   ]

_____

_____

ILLUMINATING WORDS

A number of Hebrew and Yiddish words appear in this chapter, which yield valuable insights into the life-style of Eastern European Jewry and Israel. Set down your own understanding of each of these terms, and illustrate their respective meanings with brief examples.

1. Ḥutzpah _____

_____

2. Hitnadvut_____

_____

3. Shnorrer _____

_____

4. L'histader _____

_____

5. Shlemiel_____

_____

WORD SCRAMBLE *

Unscramble the following words, and put them in an order that makes the most sense. The solution to this word scramble should give you a key insight into the nature of Israeli politics today.

1. **heret**

2. **wot**

3. **sinnipoo**

4. **wesj**

DEVIL'S ADVOCATE

The issue of religion in Israel differs from that of other democracies in that Judaism itself encompasses both a religious philosophy and a national definition. Neither of these elements can be ignored; they are active, indispensable dimensions of Jewish life as we know it. Try playing devil's advocate to both sides. Below are several arguments that have been set forth by each faction. In the blank spaces that follow, fill in whatever criticism you can think of in reply to the particular argument.

1. **Anti** (opposed to religious involvement of any kind in political affairs)

    a. A democracy must safeguard the rights of all of its citizens. What is happening here is that one faction is trying to impose its life-style upon people who do not embrace its values or beliefs.

_____

_____

_____

b. Who are they to say that their way is the only way of being Jewish? And what's worse, their way has become the law of the land. Isn't that interpreting Judaism in its narrowest possible sense?

_____

_____

_____

c. I have nothing against religion as such. And if every Jew chooses to be Orthodox, that's all right with me. But even if I happened to be Orthodox, I would passionately object to the intrusion of religious factions into political affairs. My objection is based, by the way, not upon my fear for democracy, but for religion. Democracy will survive if it's healthy to begin with, but political involvement undermines the integrity, the spirituality, of religion itself.

_____

_____

_____

d. A non-Jewish citizen of Israel is subject only to the civil authority. Israeli Jews, on the other hand, are subject to religious authority as well. Indeed, the Jews are the only people in Israel who do not enjoy complete religious freedom.

_____

_____

_____

2. **Pro** (in favor of religious involvement)

a. Jewish tradition lies at the center of our history, culture, and ethics. It must be preserved at all costs, particularly in a Jewish state.

_____

_____

_____

b. Israelis take pride in the uniqueness of who they are, and what they have done. Why can't this uniqueness extend to the sphere of religious life as well? We are both a nation and a religion. Shouldn't this be expressed, somehow, in our national life?

_____

_____

_____

c. Our traditions are, in fact, not merely symbols and ceremonies, but values. Think about the Sabbath, Pesah, Yom Kippur, Simhat Torah and the like — all of these are part of what we call the Jewish way of life, incorporating attitudes about family life, compassion, study, and freedom. Throw away religious observance (on a national scale) and our moral and ethical heritage goes right along with it. And should we really confine our values to the four walls of the synagogue? To the minutes a day of ritual observance? Shouldn't they be a part of, rather than apart from, our normal everyday existence?

_____

_____

_____

d. Israel is supposed to be the spiritual and cultural center of World Jewry. The Diaspora defines itself, philosophically and institutionally, primarily in religious terms. If we were to extract religion from our national idiom, wouldn't we, in fact, be severing our most vital links to Diaspora Jewry?

_____

_____

_____

e. Without a strong religious dimension in its makeup, Israel would not be a Jewish state but a state of Jews, a Middle Eastern country whose national language happened to be Hebrew, period! We would be divested of our mission, our memory, our larger involvements, 'a nation like every other nation,' nothing more or less. Some people call this normal, I call it assimilation on a mammoth scale.

_____

_____

_____

Chapter Twenty-Six

The Establishment

A SEARCH FOR UNDERSTANDING *

Circle the characteristic that does not fit, and in the space below, explain why.

1. Most of the veterans of Israel's establishment

    a. Know Yiddish
    b. Immigrated to Israel
    c. Believe in a particular ideology
    d. Have strong ideas as to how the country should be run
    e. Are experts in Arab customs and culture
    f. Are probably 55 years old or older

2. The Israeli establishment

    a. Is made up of relatively few people
    b. Has its origin, for the most part, in Eastern Europe
    c. Has proved reluctant to share power with the younger generation
    d. Enjoys a luxurious life-style
    e. Worries whether its successors will be faithful to the Zionist dream
    f. Has a nostalgia for, and pride in, the "good old days" of early pioneering

3. Young Israelis are most likely to achieve prominence and power in

    a. The army
    b. Kibbutzim
    c. The media
    d. Industry
    e. The arts

f. The sciences

g. The Histadrut

4. The younger Israeli leaders now coming to political power in Israel are

a. Among the oldest "Young Turks" on record
b. Veterans of at least one of Israel's wars
c. Ideologists and revolutionaries
d. Born or raised in Israel
e. Trained specialists in one field or another

5. Elderly people in Israel generally

a. Command more respect than they do in the United States
b. Are active in senior citizens groups and golden age societies
c. Do not have to worry about the rising cost of medical care
d. Are not special victims of Israel's galloping inflation
e. Know more languages than their children and grandchildren

PROBABLY TRUE OR FALSE, AND WHY? *

1. Israel's veteran settlers feel that their children have a lot to learn from the experiences of the "old days." T [　]　F [　]

_____

_____

2. Most of the members of the old Israeli establishment knew one another personally. T [　]　F [　]

_____

_____

3. An Israeli cabinet minister is as likely to be worried about paying his or her bills in the face of rising costs as anyone else. T [　]　F [　]

_____

_____

4. The old veterans opposed the introduction of television in Israel because they realized that it could assume a degree of power and influence equalling their own. T [ ] F [ ]

_____

_____

5. An American TV series that scores well in the Nielsen ratings, but whose audience is comprised largely of viewers over 60 years old, is likely to be dropped by the network. T [ ] F [ ]

_____

_____

6. Yitzḥak Rabin, the first Israeli head of government to be born in the twentieth century, was elected to office because most Israelis felt that the younger generation deserved a chance to show what it could do. T [ ] F [ ]

_____

_____

7. A 65-year-old American is likely to have many more anxieties than a 65-year-old Israeli. T [ ] F [ ]

_____

_____

8. Oriental Jews might justifiably complain that they have been completely shut out of the power structure. T [ ] F [ ]

_____

_____

WHO SAID WHAT TO WHOM? *

The place is an Israeli cafe. Sitting around a table are a veteran settler, age 74 or so; his son, in his late 40's; a native-born Israeli of Oriental extraction, age 30; an American tourist, age 55. They are engaged in a passionate discussion of — you guessed it — politics, particularly as it is practiced in Israel.

On the basis of the following conversational excerpts, try to figure out who is talking to whom, and in the spaces below, explain why. (Veteran settler=V; Son=S; Oriental Israeli=O; American tourist=A.)

1. "All right, so you fought in the War of Independence and the Sinai campaign. I'm not questioning your bravery or your patriotic commitment.

I'm just not sure that you truly grasp the ideals that have made this country what it is." [ ] to [ ]

_____

_____

2. "They're talking about a generation gap. What really bothers me is a culture gap, which in this country expresses itself in terms of political power. I'm sure you understand what I'm saying; you lived through the 1960's." [ ] to [ ]

_____

3. "You have to understand that progress — real progress, and not a bunch of symbolic trappings — comes gradually. We have had to wait our turn (sometimes the wait seemed forever), and so will you." [ ] to [ ]

_____

_____

4. "Don't get me wrong. I have a lot of respect for your generation, but somehow I feel a lot more at home, that I have a lot more in common, with the old-timers." [ ] to [ ]

_____

_____

5. "You are so steeped in the principles of your particular ideology that it is hard for you to see, and deal with, the day-to-day practical realities." [ ] to [ ]

_____

_____

6. "If you want to meet a real politician, you should meet my daughter — twenty-two, and already the treasurer of her kibbutz. One day she'll be a member of the Knesset. That's the Israeli parliament." [ ] to [ ]

_____

_____

GROWING OLDER IN A YOUTH CULTURE

The United States has long been recognized as a culture in which the overriding emphasis is upon youth. Unfortunately, the other side of the "look young, think young" coin has been the de-emphasis in many ways of the place, importance, and needs of the elderly. The categories below are general spheres in which the elderly have been penalized or discriminated against for the sin of growing old. In the spaces that follow each category, list as many specific instances of age discrimination as you can think of.

1. Income _____

_____

2. Advertising _____

_____

3. Family relationships _____

_____

4. Employment _____

_____

5. Living facilities _____

_____

6. Place in the community _____

_____

INSIGHTS

1. Why do so many elderly people, who once were members of the middle class, now live on a near poverty level income?

_____

_____

2. Why are men and women constantly warned about telltale gray? What is it that is being told, and why is this a reason for issuing a warning?

_____

_____

_____

3. Why do so many elderly people resent the fact that they are forced to retire at age 65?

_____

_____

4. Why do many older people spend their later years in nursing homes or golden age havens, rather than with their families and in the communities that they have been part of for so many years?

_____

_____

5. Why are older people special victims of inflation in this country?

_____

_____

6. Why does the rapid pace of change that characterizes today's world play particular havoc with the lives of the elderly?

_____

_____

CASE IN POINT

Do you know of any older people who have become victims of our youth culture — for any of the reasons noted above, or because of other factors? If so, tell their story in a paragraph or two, including what you believe to be the specific causes of their situation.

Chapter Twenty-Seven

Life on the Kibbutz

THE KIBBUTZ LIFE-STYLE

Imagine that you have decided to go on aliyah to Israel, and to make a life for yourself on the kibbutz. Your parents are upset. They do not oppose your settling in Israel; indeed, they are proud of your decision to express your Jewish identity and commitment in such a manner. But the kibbutz is something else again. It means that you will never have money, never have a career, never have the opportunity to be a success in any conventional sense. In brief, life on a kibbutz seems to fly in the face of many of the aims and achievements that they have valued all of their lives.

You want to clear up your parent's misconceptions, to persuade them that the kibbutz has values and satisfactions that are at least as worthy as the life-style that you are giving up. How, then would you answer the following questions and criticisms?

1. You'll never have any money, any security. You'll be a pauper all of your life.

   _____

   _____

   _____

2. All of your friends are going into medicine, law, business, education. And you are going to let your talents go to waste! Working as a laborer on a farm!

   _____

   _____

   _____

3. What kind of a family life can you have, with your children being raised by other people, and not living in the same house with you?

   _____

   _____

   _____

4. All right, you are young now, and don't mind hardship and austerity. But how about when you are older? How will a life of roughing it appeal to you then, when it is too late to make a change?

_____

_____

_____

5. You may not realize it, but a number of social and cultural activities have become part of your life — books, films, plays, music, stimulating discussions, and the like. Where will you find all of this on a farming community?

_____

_____

_____

ATTITUDES AND VALUES

What kibbutz values are expressed by the following descriptions? At times, the description in question might express several values; at other times, one value might play a role in several areas of kibbutz activity.

1. The absence of money as a medium of exchange, and as a criterion of status and individual quality.

_____

_____

2. Settlements in the Negev, and on Israel's borders.

_____

_____

3. The establishment of kibbutz ulpanim (intensive Hebrew language seminars) and work-study programs for visiting Jews from abroad.

_____

_____

4. The policy of sending those members who so desire to study at a university. (A kibbutznik may have to wait his or her turn, but will eventually be given the opportunity.)

_____

_____

5. The fact that the traditional first question asked by kibbutzniks about newcomers (both visitors and candidates for membership) is, "How conscientiously do they work?"

_____

_____

6. The fact that two members who joined the kibbutz at the same time are treated entirely equally in terms of housing, vacations, food, clothing, medical care, and assorted benefits, although Member A has been dramatically more capable and contributing than Member B.

_____

_____

7. The fact that kibbutzim do not integrate socially, economically, or culturally with their immediate rural or semirural environment.

_____

_____

8. The fact that newcomers to the kibbutz invariably feel that every face turns to stare when they enter the kibbutz dining room for the first time.

_____

_____

9. The fact that kibbutz members make up so disproportionately high a percentage of soldiers in frontline military units, and account for so many battle casualties.

_____

_____

10. The fact that the kibbutzim have generally made a point of creating a physically pleasant and culturally stimulating environment for their members.

_____

_____

11. The fact that truly dedicated kibbutzniks object to the practice of families' eating their evening meals in their apartments, rather than in the kibbutz dining room.

_____

_____

12. The ability of the kibbutzim to bend and redefine old ideological ground rules, to adapt to changing times and members' growing needs (e.g.,

diversifying their economy; employing hired labor, particularly from among the new Oriental immigrants; modifying living arrangements — in a number of kibbutzim today, children live with their parents, rather than in children's houses).

AN INVENTORY OF SKILLS

Imagine a 12-year-old kibbutz located in the Western Galilee, about 20 miles north of Haifa, 3 miles from the Lebanese border, and touching the shores of the Mediterranean. Like every kibbutz, it has its sizable contingents of cows and chickens, and the various products that can be derived from these two species. In addition, assorted vegetables (carrots, radishes, tomatoes, and sugar beets) are grown. Bananas and peanuts have become major industries.

There is a Youth Aliyah children's village on its premises, with 50 to 100 teenagers who must be educated, counseled, integrated (on a part-time basis) into the kibbutz work force, taught a trade, or prepared for further study. The kibbutzniks (some 700 in all) range in age from about 25 to 40. Most of their children are of school age, and the birthrate shows no signs of dropping in the near future. Many of the veteran members live in well-appointed two-room apartments, but there is a good deal of building to be done before all of the permanent housing is completed. The grounds surrounding the living area are attractive, but by no means developed. And just last year, the kibbutz opened a furniture factory that shows every sign of being a huge success.

Given the above profile, make a list below of different skills necessary to keep this kibbutz happy, healthy, and effectively functioning on a day-to-day basis. (For example, the furniture factory needs woodcutters, bookkeepers, loaders, designers, and carpenters.)

CONTRASTS

For all of its expansion into new areas such as industries and crafts, the kibbutz is still, at core, a farming operation. What are some of the major differences between the kibbutz and a community of small farmers in this country? Each of the statements below describes one aspect of life, either on the kibbutz or on an American farm. Complete each statement as best you can.

1. The average American small farmer is engaged in this occupation either because he happens to like the work, or because he was born into it; the average kibbutznik

   _____

   _____

   _____

2. The American small farmer lives at the edge of insecurity in the sense that he is at the mercy of elements beyond his control (climate, prices, etc.); the kibbutznik

   _____

   _____

   _____

3. The American farm family is a self-contained unit, most often living considerable distances from its neighbors; kibbutz families

   _____

   _____

   _____

4. The kibbutz is often characterized as "an island of culture"; most American farming communities

_____

_____

5. An American farmer would be likely to leave his land for but one reason, inability to make a living; a kibbutznik might decide to pull up stakes for a variety of reasons, including

_____

_____

6. The majority of American farm communities are politically conservative; Israeli kibbutzim

_____

_____

_____

INSIGHTS

1. Why are kibbutzniks described as "a nobility of service"?

_____

_____

2. Why would someone trained as a physician be one of the most likely candidates to leave a kibbutz eventually?

_____

_____

3. Why might someone with many personal problems be attracted by kibbutz life?

_____

_____

4. Why is there so high a percentage of kibbutz members involved in the political life of the nation?

_____

_____

_____

5. Why do kibbutzniks usually marry other kibbutzniks?

_____

_____

_____

6. Why does "intermarriage" with a nonkibbutznik often cause such a couple to leave the kibbutz entirely?

_____

_____

_____

7. Why has the kibbutz, whose numbers have never exceeded 8 percent of Israel's total population, exerted so powerful an influence upon the attitudes and values of the Jewish state?

_____

_____

_____

_____

8. Why do you think that the kibbutz has managed to take root and flourish, while so many other efforts to create an ideal or utopian community have failed?

_____

_____

_____

_____

THE MEANING OF SUCCESS

Anyone who decides to live on a kibbutz has, in effect, given up the pursuit of success as it is generally understood in most Western societies today. To put it another way, the kibbutznik defines success in radically different terms from what most of us are used to.

1. Briefly sum up what success means to you.

2. Who is the most successful individual you know, and why?

3. If you were granted three wishes determining how you will live the rest of your life, what would they be in order of their importance to you?

    a. _____

    _____

    b. _____

    _____

    c. _____

    _____

Chapter Twenty-Eight

In a Small Country

PROBABLY TRUE OR FALSE, AND WHY? *

1. If the Middle East were not considered an area of vital interest by outside powers, the Arab-Israeli conflict might have been resolved years ago. T [ ] F [ ]

   _____

   _____

2. The Soviet Union wanted to see the Middle East erupt into a series of all-out wars during its years of involvement. T [ ] F [ ]

   _____

   _____

3. Israeli history clearly demonstrates that morality and justice play a decisive role in international affairs. T [ ] F [ ]

   _____

   _____

4. Despite serious problems along the way, the process of immigrant absorption in Israel has been notably successful. T [ ] F [ ]

   _____

   _____

5. An Israeli might well say to a tourist, "Forget all the things that you have read and heard about the sabras. These are stereotypes, distortions, that don't begin to tell you who we really are." T [ ] F [ ]

   _____

   _____

6. The very smallness of Israel (in terms of both territory and population) threatens to undermine its democracy. T [ ] F [ ]

   _____

   _____

7. Israelis are singularly likely to be suspicious of the world at large.
   T [ ] F [ ]

   _____

   _____

   _____

THE LESSONS OF HISTORY *

Israel is a nation for whom history has been an active, sustained, and sustaining point of reference over the years. Match the historical events in the left column with the lessons that they teach in the right column.

1. The Dreyfus trial

   _____ Power and self-interest is the name of the game in global politics; for Israel to seek support on moral grounds alone is almost inevitably doomed to disappointment.

2. The Warsaw Ghetto uprising

   _____ In the proper setting, idealism can be a powerful force, an active social value.

3. The development of the kibbutz life–style

   _____ A society that is deeply motivated and committed often has the capacity to do what any expert would call the impossible.

4. The Holocaust

   _____ Will, passion, and desperation are factors that must be taken into account in a battle as surely as manpower and weaponry.

5. Israel's isolation in the international community after the Yom Kippur War

   _____ Political emancipation of the Jewish people, and enlightened legislation that protects their rights, are, in themselves, not cures for anti-Semitism and its effects.

6. The modern Ingathering of _____ Man's inhumanity to man,
Exiles into the state of Israel when unleashed (often under the banner of God,
country, or noble cause),
knows no limits.

MEANINGS

Each of the excerpts below have been taken directly from the text. Rewrite
them in a way that they will be understandable to someone who knows
nothing either of Jewish history or of Israel.

1. "Memory, a main source of inspiration for Zionism, remains one of
Israel's major emotional resources today."

_____

_____

_____

2. "The girl soldier with a submachine gun in one hand and a volume of
philosophy in the other is as false an image as the 'crooked-nosed
businessman' of old. . . ."

_____

_____

_____

3. "We saw how men fired by a messianic idea of redemption ended up by
'playing the game of the world'."

_____

_____

_____

4. "There is among Israelis today an emotional, almost tribal sense of
sticking together which sometimes puzzles outsiders."

_____

_____

_____

5. "Herzl was right, generally speaking, when he predicted that in the
future Jewish state, the individual would neither be crushed between

the millstones of capitalism nor cut down by the leveling pressure of socialism."

_____

_____

_____

6. "When asked if he thought there would be peace, David Ben-Gurion answered that peace would come whenever the U.S. and the U.S.S.R. decided that *they* wanted peace, and not before."

_____

_____

_____

_____

ATLAS OF TWENTIETH-CENTURY JEWISH HISTORY

The map opposite includes various locations in which events and developments of major significance to Jewish history have taken place. The following are descriptions of those events and developments. Place the number next to the description alongside the appropriate location that is noted on the map. (Not every location on the map is described below.)

1. The location of the first Zionist Congress.
2. The ancient port through which most of the early Zionist pioneers entered Palestine.
3. The country that lost the greatest number of Jews during the Holocaust.
4. The island on which many Jewish illegal immigrants who were caught by the British authorities were interned, in the years between World War II and the creation of Israel.
5. The country from which "Operation Magic Carpet," one of the most dramatic chapters in the story of the Ingathering of the Exiles, took place.
6. The city in which Theodor Herzl was shocked into Zionism.
7. The city whose name was affixed to the oppressive laws enacted by the Nazi regime to limit the movements, actions, and options of German Jews.
8. The city from which the Balfour Declaration was issued.
9. The city in Eastern Europe that was one of the great centers of Jewish culture and learning before the Holocaust.
10. The country (in the Diaspora) that has the second largest Jewish population in the world today.

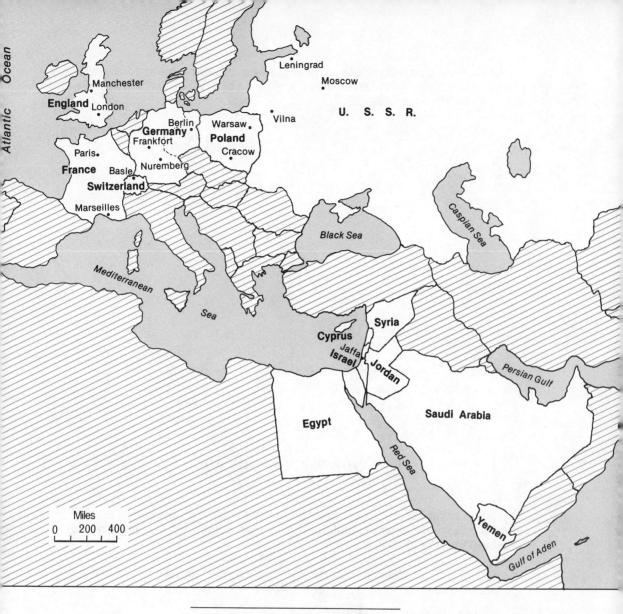

A PUBLIC RELATIONS MEMO

Most observers (Israelis included) agree that the Arabs have proved to be far more energetic and adept at public relations than have the Israelis. They have poured enormous amounts of time, talent, and money into their propaganda apparatus, for the express purpose of promoting their cause in the eyes of the world. And Israel, for a variety of reasons, and to the dismay of many of its supporters, has responded neither in quality nor in kind. Imagine that you have been charged with the task of mapping out a public relations campaign in your community for Israel. No outright lies, no distortions of facts or issues are needed; the truth is sufficient, provided that the presentation is planned with the idea of creating general support for Israel's position. What points of Israeli history, policy, etc., would you want to see emphasized in such a campaign?

ODD PERSON OUT *

Circle the letter before the section that does *not* fit the meaning of each of the following statements, and in the spaces below, briefly explain the reason(s) for your choice.

1. If you probed the consciousness of the average Israeli, you would be likely to find

   a. Anxiety over the future
   b. A strong sense of history
   c. Suspicion of the outside world
   d. Irritation over the stereotypes of Israelis that are regularly projected by the media
   e. A sense of outrage over the ever-growing economic distance between the Israeli haves and have-nots
   f. A deep-down awareness that Israel will have to extend itself still further, when the next problem or crisis appears upon the landscape of Jewish life

   _____

   _____

2. An early Zionist pioneer surveying the contemporary Israeli scene might

   a. Say of the Russians, "If it isn't one thing, it's another; they are always making trouble for us"
   b. Take pride in many of Israel's social institutions
   c. Feel that modern Israel bears no resemblance at all to the original Zionist blueprint
   d. Reflect that sovereign statehood has neither decreased the isolation of the Jewish people, nor prevented them from being singled out as victims of prejudice and hatred
   e. Take comfort in the fact that Israel is, and always will be, a small country

   _____

   _____

3. A French politician might

   a. Feel embarrassed in private conversation with his Israeli counterparts
   b. Publicly accuse Israel of aggression and intransigence
   c. Go to great lengths to avoid incurring Arab displeasure
   d. Believe that his country's Middle East policy has been consistent since 1948
   e. Try to persuade French Jewish voters that they must place the interests of France above the interests of a foreign government, lest they be accused of dual loyalty

   _____

   _____

4. An American Jewish tourist with relatively little background visiting Israel for the first time might

   a. Wonder why Israeli girls look so unmuscular
   b. Feel that Israel is just a Middle Eastern version of his Jewish community back home
   c. Be amazed at the variety of unfamiliar Jewish types whom he has come across
   d. Want to attend an ulpan when he returns home
   e. Discover a sense of connection with his ancient past
   f. Feel a surge of identification and involvement with the Jewish state

   _____

   _____

Unit Seven
Understanding the Jewish State

Chapter Twenty-Nine

A Jewish State

ISSUES IN DEPTH

Support the following general statements with references to, or excerpts from, the text.

1. Because of its nature and special responsibilities, a Jewish state can never be truly normal.

   _____

   _____

   _____

2. Israel has the odds heavily stacked against it in the sphere of international diplomacy.

   _____

   _____

   _____

3. Seen in logical (as opposed to political) perspective, the charge that Zionism is a form of racism can be easily, and decisively, refuted.

   _____

   _____

   _____

4. The Law of Return is Israel's response to the realities of Jewish history.

   _____

   _____

   _____

5. The settlers of the Yishuv believed that morality took precedence over official law, and were willing to translate this view into concrete actions.

   _____

_____

_____

6. Defining one's Jewish identity can be more problematic than, say, defining one's Catholic identity.

_____

_____

_____

7. Proof of the horrors of the Holocaust did not deter British policy makers from going about their business as usual.

_____

_____

_____

_____

TRUE OR FALSE? *

1. Israel, though a small, poor country, is steeped in science and technology. T [ ] F [ ]

2. The chief rabbis of Israel are recognized as Judaism's highest religious authorities throughout the world. T [ ] F [ ]

3. Great Britain exercised a policy of restricting Jewish immigration from the time it became the mandatory power in Palestine after World War I. T [ ] F [ ]

4. The clash between religionists and secularists in Israel is one that will not be easily resolved by negotiation, or even by compromise. T [ ] F [ ]

5. The problem of defining Jewish identity arose in the wake of emancipation from the European ghetto, because Jews began to think of themselves as citizens of their countries-of origin, and accordingly, to lose sight of their ancient national roots. T [ ] F [ ]

6. Israel's policy of serving as a haven for Jews everywhere has been attacked as a form of racism. T [ ] F [ ]

7. One of the aims of the early Zionists was to stem the tides of Jewish assimilation the world over. T [ ] F [ ]

8. With the existence of the State of Israel, assimilation has ceased being a threat to Jewish life. T [ ] F [ ]

INSIGHTS

1. Why does Solomon Schechter dread assimilation even more than pogroms?

   _____

   _____

2. Why does Judah Magnes believe that "the Land is one of the chief means, if not the chief means, of revitalizing the people and the Torah"?

   _____

   _____

3. Why did the British government refuse to change its restrictive immigration policy even in the face of overwhelming evidence of the destruction of European Jewry?

   _____

   _____

4. Why was Aliyah Bet so named?

   _____

   _____

5. Why has religion become a political issue in Israel today?

   _____

   _____

6. Why was Zionism condemned as a form of racism in the UN General Assembly?

   _____

   _____

7. Why is Israel's smallness (both in terms of geography and population) considered a source of potential danger?

   _____

   _____

   _____

8. Why did the question of Jewish identity become a problem with Jewish emancipation from the ghettos of Europe in the early nineteenth century?

_____

_____

_____

WHERE JUDAISM DIFFERS

You have a Christian friend who has heard that Judaism cannot be defined in the same terms as other religions. "A Catholic who is an atheist no longer considers himself a Catholic," he declares, "but a Jewish atheist or agnostic may well continue to think of himself as a committed Jew, and act accordingly—embrace Zionism, feel a sense of involvement with other Jews, be an active part of the community. Frankly, I don't get it. From where I stand the whole thing just doesn't make sense. What *is* a Jew? How do you define Jewish identity? How, and why, is Judaism different from other religions?"

How would you answer these questions? In the space below, put down as many differences as you can think of between Judaism and other religions. Or, in your own words, try to formulate an explanation of the nature of Jewish identity that will clear up your Christian friend's confusion.

WORD SCRAMBLE *

Unscramble the following words, each of which has served at one time or another as a contributing factor in the process of assimilation, losing one's Jewish identity. Then, unscramble the circled letters to discover what many Jews feel is the crucial component in the fight against assimilation.

1. surycintie

2. boitmain

3. nagroince

4. woceidrac

5. hemas

ISRAEL'S JEWISH IDENTITY

Which aspects of its Jewish identity has Israel expressed through the following actions and policies?

1. Aliyah Bet _____

_____

2. The Law of Return _____

_____

3. The Eichmann trial_____

_____

4. Its preoccupation with archaeology _____

_____

5. The distinction that it makes in its law between "Jewish" and other nationals _____

_____

6. The growing political power of Orthodox Judaism _____

_____

7. The strong involvement with, and attachment to, a life on the land (the kibbutz, the moshav, the independent farm, etc.)

_____

_____

8. The various institutions of social welfare that exist in Israel

_____

ESTABLISHING PRIORITIES

Jews have expressed their identity in many ways over the years. Below is a sampling of such expressions. Number them in what you consider to be their order of importance.

_____ Going to synagogue on the Sabbath

_____ Visiting Israel

_____ Studying a portion of the Torah each week

_____ Playing an active role in the affairs of your synagogue, temple, or Jewish communal life in general

_____ Creating an intense Jewish environment in your home

_____ Working in behalf of persecuted Jews in the Soviet Union and other countries

_____ Getting involved in social action programs in the community

_____ Joining the Zionist movement

_____ Going on aliyah to Israel

_____ Helping the Jewish poor and aged in your own community

Briefly discuss what the order you have chosen reveals about your Jewish values and priorities.

COMBATING ASSIMILATION

You are put in charge of a group of Jewish boys and girls who have had no Jewish background, no Jewish education, no Jewish involvement. Their feelings about Judaism range from indifference to outright distaste. They see Judaism, at best, as a relic from their grandparents' generation, and often as a source of embarrassment and restriction. ("Why do I have to marry another Jew? People are people whatever their background. What you are asking is a form of discrimination.") Your job is to halt the process of assimilation, to instill in them a sense of Jewish awareness, involvement, and pride. How would you go about doing it?

In a paragraph, briefly outline the steps of an anti-assimilationist strategy that you think might work with them.

Chapter Thirty

What Does the Future Hold?

ISRAEL'S UNIQUE CHARACTER

In the first chapter of *Understanding Israel*, the point was made that in a number of spheres, Israel is unique — definitively set apart in terms of experiences, self-definition, and aims — from other nations.

Explain how each of the following is a concrete expression of Israel's unique character.

1. The return to the land

2. The rebirth of Hebrew as a living language

3. The religious issue in Israel

4. The creation of the kibbutz

5. Aliyah Bet

6. The Law of Return

_____

_____

_____

7. The nature of Israel's conflict with its Arab neighbors

_____

_____

_____

8. The presence of shliḥim and ulpanim, sponsored by Israel, in various Diaspora communities today

_____

_____

_____

9. The Holocaust as an active element in Israeli feeling and thought

_____

_____

10. Various definitions of Jewish identity today

_____

_____

_____

MEANINGS

The text refers to three famous quotations (listed below) to sum up the meaning of modern Zionism. On the basis of what you have learned in this course, discuss how each of these ideas was specifically xpressed in the process of Israel's creation.

1. "If I am not for myself, who then is for me?"

_____

_____

_____

2. "We came to build the land and to be rebuilt by it. . . ."

_____

_____

_____

_____

3. "If you will it, it is no legend."

_____

_____

_____

THE ZIONIST REVOLUTION

The statements below are descriptions that could have been made about Jewish life in the early 1900's. In the spaces that follow, rewrite each statement in terms of the situation of Israel and world Jewry today. This should help crystallize the nature and direction of the Zionist revolution, and the difference that it has made.

1. Hebrew can best be characterized as Lashon HaKadesh ("the Holy Tongue") truly understood only by a religious or cultural elite. The overwhelming majority of Jews speak Yiddish, Ladino, or the languages of their respective countries of origin.

2. Hebrew literature is an intellectual exercise practiced by the educated few.

3. The Jewish people have no power base except insofar as they are able to wield a degree of influence in those countries that have granted them political rights.

4. The Jewish people, particularly those who lived in the shtetl and other ghettos (physical or psychological), have a different sense of time from the rest of the world. Their primary points of reference are the biblical past and the messianic future; they view the present (whenever that happens to be) as a holding action whose primary aime are to preserve (the past) and to prepare (for the future).

5. The Jew is like the proverbial fiddler on the roof: homeless, rootless, perpetually poised for flight, hoping that his next address will offer a measure of peacefulness and security, at least for a while.

6. The Jewish people, living as they do on the fringes of other peoples' societies, are helpless, dependent upon the will and whim of the majority for their well-being. They can barely help themselves, much less each other.

7. The Jews are alienated and abnormal, primarily restricted to middleman positions and the professions, and with little relationship with the land itself.

ISRAEL'S VALUES

Below are some of the values that have been incorporated into Israeli life over the years. In the space beside each value, give one or two examples of how it has been translated into a specific action, achievement, or national policy.

1. A relationship with the past   _____

                                              _____

                                              _____

2. A sense of connection with the land   _____

                                              _____

3. A yearning for self-sufficiency   _____

                                              _____

4. An identification with Jewish suffering   _____

                                              _____

                                              _____

5. Concern for justice and equality   _____

                                              _____

6. Involvement with, and commitment to, world Jewry   _____

                                              _____

7. The need to lead a complete Jewish life   _____

                                              _____

8. A view of idealism, not as an occasional or sentimental point of reference, but as an active and central value in its own right   _____

                                              _____

IN THE YEAR 2000

In a paragraph or so, set forth the vision of Israel and world Jewry that you would like to see come to pass in the year 2000.

Answer Key

This workbook has two kinds of questions: those which may be answered by reference to facts and data in the textbook, and those which require the student to reorganize and evaluate the material being studied. The following Key provides answers *only* for those questions which are factual in nature.

Chapter One

GENERAL KNOWLEDGE *(page 4)*

1. May 14, 1948   2. David Ben-Gurion   3. Moshe Sharett, Levi Eshkol, Golda Meir, Yitzhak Rabin, and Menahem Begin   4. Chaim Weizmann   5. Theodor Herzl   6. Four   7. The War of Independence (1948), The Sinai Campaign (1956), The Six Day War (1967), The Yom Kippur War (1973)   8. (c) 1961   9. (c) Iraq   10. Halutz   11. Kibbutz   12. (b) ascent   13. c; d; e; a; b   14. (b) Jerusalem   15. (c) 3 million   16. False

WORD SCRAMBLE *(page 7)*

1. Negev   2. Herzl   3. Haifa   4. Jewish   5. Horah   6. Jerusalem   Circled letters: Zionism

Chapter Two

A SEARCH FOR UNDERSTANDING *(page 8)*

1. (d) nonpolitical   3. False   4. e; f; a; b; d; c   6. (b) Rachel Yanait Ben-Zvi

IDENTIFICATION *(page 9)*

1. Czar   2. Sabra   3. Degania   4. Sdeh Boker   5. Diaspora   6. Pogrom   7. Uganda

WHO AM I? *(page 12)*

1. Petah Tikvah   2. Cossack   3. Socialism   4. Jaffa   5. Leshanah Haba'ah Bi-rushalayim

Chapter Three

COMPONENTS OF THE ZIONIST REVOLUTION

True or False? *(page 15)*

a. False   b. True   c. True   d. False   e. True

WORD SCRAMBLE *(page 16)*

1. of a own our land = A land of our own   2. Jews a haven for = A haven for Jews   3. From anti-Semitism freedom = Freedom from anti-Semitism   4. Hebrew revival of = Revival of Hebrew   5. just a society Jewish = A just Jewish society

---

Chapter Four

A SEARCH FOR UNDERSTANDING *(page 20)*

1. (c) Israel's desire for a united Jerusalem   2. (e) Improved prospects for Arab-Israeli peace   4. (d) They are threatened with national destruction   6. (a) The Soviet Union's long-standing tradition of anti-Semitism   7. (b) Arab territory captured by Israel during the Six Day War   8. False

MAP STUDY *(page 22)*

1. True   2. (d) Jordan   3a. W   3b. S   3c. G   3d. W   3e. S   3f. W   4a. Kuneitra   4b. Eilat   4c. Hebron, Sh'chem (called Nablus by the Arabs)   4d. Gaza   4e. Sharm el Sheikh

HISTORY'S HEADLINES *(page 24)*

1. The Sinai Campaign   2. The War of Independence   3. The Yom Kippur War   4. The Six Day War   5. The Sinai Campaign   6. The Yom Kippur War   7. The War of Attrition   8. The Six Day War   9. The War of Independence   10. The Six Day War

---

Chapter Five

MATCHING DESCRIPTIONS *(page 28)*

4; 6; 1; 2; 3   Der goldene medine (5) is the term with no matching description.

TRUE OR FALSE? *(page 30)*

1. False (There were far more, roughly 7 million Jews.)   2. True   3. True   4. False   5. False

CREATIVE RESPONSES *(page 30)*

1. The development of Yiddish literature   2. Modern Zionism, culminating in the creation of the State of Israel   3. The rebirth of Hebrew as a living language and the beginnings of modern Hebrew literature   4. The establishment of a strong American Jewish community   5. The kibbutz

Chapter Six

A SEARCH FOR UNDERSTANDING *(page 35)*

1. (c) Accepting the situation and making the best of it   2. BILU; "House of Jacob, come and let us go"   3. False   5. (f) Had nothing in common with the Zionist movement   6. (c) Foresaw a time when Jews would be free, fulfilled, and unafraid wherever they lived

A SCRAMBLED STORY *(page 36)*

Here are the words in their appropriate order: escaping;   Diaspora;   radicalism;   identity;   Zionists;   homelend;   permanence

A THREE-WAY DISCUSSION *(page 38)*

1. R to Z   2. I to R   3. Z to I   4. I to Z   5. Z to R

Chapter Seven

A SEARCH FOR UNDERSTANDING *(page 40)*

pogrom;   aliens;   "cultured" Russians;   incurable disease;   Auto-Emancipation — An Appeal to His People by a Russian Jew;   The lovers of Zion;   Palestine;   national poet;   will to live

WHO SAID WHAT? *(page 42)*

1. P   2. L   3. B   4. L   5. J   6. P   7. B   8. P

YIDDISH HUMOR *(page 43)*

1. "The *shlemiel* lands on his back and bruises his nose."   2. "A man should live, if only to satisfy his own curiosity."   3. "One father supports ten children, but ten children do not support one father."   4. "Shrouds are made without pockets."   5. "God loves the poor, but He helps the rich."

Chapter Eight

A SEARCH FOR UNDERSTANDING *(page 44)*

1. (e) Prepared for every problem that came their way   2. (b) Jaffa
3. c; d; a; b   4. False   5. False

MAP STUDY *(page 46)*

1. Jerusalem   2. Tiberias   2a. Kinneret   3. Safed   4. Petaḥ Tikvah
5. Jaffa

WORD SCRAMBLE *(page 49)*

1. Jaffa 2. Farming 3. Idealism 4. Pioneer Circled letters:
Freedom

Chapter Nine

MOTIVATIONS *(page 50)*

3; 4; 2; 1

PLACES ON THE MAP *(page 50)*

1. Petaḥ Tikvah 2. Zichron Yaakov 3. Rishon le-Zion 5. Rosh
Pinnah 5. Hadera

FAMILY RELATIONSHIPS *(Page 54)*

The four families are: 1. (book) סֵפֶר (library) סִפְרִיָּה (author) סוֹפֵר
(school) בֵּית־סֵפֶר 2. (order) סֵדֶר (prayerbook) סִדּוּר (organizer) סַדְרָן
(formation; parade) מִסְדָּר 3. (go) הוֹלֵךְ (process) תַּהֲלִיךְ (Jewish Law,
which instructs a Jew how to live or proceed in terms of the sacred
tradition) הֲלָכָה (journey) מַהֲלָךְ 4. (pass) עוֹבֵר (transition) מַעֲבָר
(side) עֵבֶר (transfer) הַעֲבָרָה

Chapter Ten

PINPOINT THE OUTSIDER *(page 58)*

1. (d) He believed that the fact that the Jewish people were able to remain
religiously and culturally intact (and apart from other peoples) for 2000
years entitled them to a state of their own 2. (b) The introduction of the
idea that the Jews were a nation as well as a religious group 3. (e) A man
who thoroughly understood Judaism and the Jewish people 4. (c) Was a
conspiracy hatched by anti-Semites to demonstrate that French Jews were
subversive outsiders, and should not be regarded as citizens and patriots
5. (c) Cut itself off completely from Jewish communities in the Diaspora

EVENTS AND EFFECTS *(page 60)*

5; 4; 1; 6; 3; 2

HISTORY'S HEADLINES *(page 62)*

1a. Emile Zola's libel conviction, because of his defense of Dreyfus
1b. French Jews were dismissed from their jobs, as part of the "guilt by
generalization" wave that swept France in the wake of the Dreyfus
Affair 1c. The publication of *The Jewish State* 1d. The young pioneers
of the Second Aliyah versus the older Biluim 1e. A Young Zionist going
on aliyah 1f. The first World Zionist Congress 1g. Alfred Dreyfus,
finally pardoned and reinstated in the French army 1h. One brother
immigrates to the United States; the other to Palestine

Chapter Eleven

TRUE OR FALSE, AND WHY? *(page 65)*

Here are the true or false answers; you explain why.   1. True   2. False
3. True   4. True   5. False   6. True

THE LANGUAGE OF IDEALISM *(page 66)*

3;   4;   5;   2;   1

Chapter Twelve

NAMES AND THEIR MEANINGS *(page 72)*

1. Herzliah   2. Shimshoni   3. Tikvah   4. Ben Aharon   5. Yizraelah
6. Balfouriah   7. T'nuvah   8. Alon

ATTITUDES AND VALUES *(page 73)*

(5) A desire to keep alive memories of Jewish ghetto life in the Diaspora

Chapter Thirteen

ODD IDEA OUT *(page 78)*

1. (c) Everyone tells me about my obligations to my parents, my rabbi, the
local authorities, the Jewish people. When I go to Palestine, I'll only be
responsible to and for myself; no one will tell me what to do.   2. (d) The
individual is nothing; the group, everything.   3. (a) The permanent
separation of body and spirit.

EDITORIAL CRITICISMS *(page 80)*

3;   5;   4;   1;   2

Chapter Fourteen

A SEARCH FOR UNDERSTANDING *(page 85)*

Hashomer;   new settlements;   within the community;   hired Arab
guards;   Biluim;   fighting;   Haganah;   self-sufficiency;   Labor
Brigade;   roads;   pride and prestige;   physical labor;   kibbutz;
vitality

MAP STUDY *(page 87)*

1. Tel Aviv to Haifa   2. Beersheba to Eilat   3. Tel Aviv to Jerusalem
4. Beersheba to Sodom   5. Sodom to Masada   6. Haifa to Safed
7. Tiberias to Metullah

PROBABLY TRUE OR FALSE? *(page 88)*

Here are the true or false answers; you explain why.   1. False   2. True
3. True   4. False   5. True   6. False

Chapter Fifteen

WHO (OR WHAT) AM I? *(page 90)*

1. Meir Yaari   2. An American cowboy   3. Passover   4. The
Diaspora   5. Eddah   6. Hashomer Hatzair   7. Siḥah

VANTAGE POINTS *(page 91)*

2;   4;   1;   5;   3

WORD SCRAMBLE *(page 94)*

1. Eddah   2. Commune   3. Siḥah   4. Passion   5. Charismatic
Circled letters: Utopia

Chapter Sixteen

A SEARCH FOR UNDERSTANDING *(page 98)*

1. 1943;   Holocaust;   Philistine;   Gaza Strip (1947 Egyptian border)
2. Mordechai Anilevicz;   Warsaw Ghetto uprising;   Egyptian;   six;
line;   defense;   destruction   3. 24;   "Molotov cocktails";   last man;
rebuilt;   water tower   4. 60,000;   extermination   5. resistance;
Passover;   28;   synagogue   6. Burma Road;   Jerusalem;   supply;
Judean hills

HISTORY'S HEADLINES *(page 99)*

1. Founding of Ashkelon in 1953   2. Nazi insistence that Jews deported
from the Warsaw Ghetto were sent to work (rather than death) camps
3. The beginning of the Warsaw Ghetto uprising   4. The teacher in
question broke the laws of the concentration camp by scratching Hebrew
letters on the ground, so that the children could learn to read   5. The
building of the Burma Road   6. Disputes between factions in the Warsaw
Ghetto, over whether to cooperate with the Nazis (in the hope of buying
survival time), or to resist   7. The invasion of Israel by armies of
neighboring Arab states in May 1948   8. The defense of Yad Mordechai

ENEMY EDITORIALS *(page 100)*

1. [4]   2. [7]   3. [1]   4. [8]   5. [2]   6. [5]   7. [3]   8. [6]

Chapter Seventeen

OFFICIAL STATEMENTS (page 106)

3; 4; 5; 1; 2

ODD PERSON, IDEA, OR EVENT OUT (page 109)

1. (h) A lawyer   2. (d) The settlement in Israel of refugees from the Holocaust, and later, from a number of Arab countries   3. (c) The fear of unemployment   4. (a)Nazi concentration camps   5. (c) They hoped to make peace with Israel from a position of strength, and on their terms

Chapter Eighteen

REMEMBERING THE HOLOCAUST (page 112)

1. 1933-1945 2. National Socialist   3. *Mein Kampf*   4. False (They won the national elections.)   5. (c) (Chamberlain's appeasement policy was formulated five years after the Nazis came to power.)   6. The Weimar Republic   7. The Third Reich, sometimes called the Thousand Year Reich, on the basis of the belief that Nazi Germany would last 1000 years   8. (a) Heinrich Himmler — head of the elite SS;   (b) Joseph Goebbels — in charge of propaganda;   (c) Hermann Goering — head of the Luftwaffe, etc.;   (d) Joachim von Ribbentrop — Foreign Minister;   (e) Albert Speer — Munitions Minister   9. Axis, Allies   10. Benito Mussolini and Hideki Tojo (Prime Minister of Japan; the Emperor Hirohito was the head of state)   11. Ethiopia   12. False (World War II began in September 1939, when Great Britain and France went to war against Germany. The United States, partly because of internal politics and strong isolationist sentiment, did not enter the war against Germany until more than two years later, when the Japanese attacked Pearl Harbor.)   13. Munich 14. Czechoslovakia   15. (d) Germany invaded Poland   16.   (b) Sweden 17. Master, Aryan   18. Final Solution   19. Der Sturmer   20. (c) Poland 21. (a) Hamburg   22. True   23. Denmark   24. Genocide

TRUE OR FALSE? (page 114)

1. False   2. True   3. True   4. True   5. False   6. False   7. True 8. True   9. False   10. False

IDENTIFY THE FOLLOWING (page 116)

1. Yad Vashem   2. Armenians   3. Haj Amin el-Husseini, the grand mufti of Jerusalem   4. The Jewish Brigade   5. Poland, Lithuania, Hungary, Latvia, and Rumania, among others   6. The White Paper 7. Parachutists   8. The Eichmann Trial

Chapter Twenty

THE SABRA IN PERSPECTIVE *(page 130)*

1. The sabra is the name of a cactus fruit that grows in Israel — prickly on the outside, sweet on the inside   2. (e) The frustrations of being a religious minority   3. (c) To win acceptance in international high society   4. False

WHO SAID WHAT? *(page 132)*

2; 5; 6; 1; 4; 3

AGES AND EVENTS *(page 134)*

1. a; b; f; j; l; m   2. a; b; d; f; h; j; l; m   3. d; e; g; h; k   4. c; d; g; i; k   5. c; i; k

WORD SCRAMBLE *(page 136)*

1. Hatred   2. Hebrew   3. Bible   4. Land   5. Immigrant   6. Tourist   7. Battle   8. Tension   Circled letters: Hidden emotions

Chapter Twenty-One

VALUES AND THEIR PROBLEMS *(page 140)*

5; 3; 1; 2; 4

Chapter Twenty-Two

WHO SAID WHAT? *(page 144)*

Here are the answers; you explain why.   1. G   2. G   3. S   4. G   5. S   6. S   7. G   8. S

WORDS AND ATTITUDES *(page 145)*

4; 5; 2; 1; 3

POLITICS AND POETRY *(page 147)*

1. "Tomorrow. . . the old battleships will glisten with the gold of oranges. . ."   2. "All this will happen tomorrow, if not today; it is as clear as the light at noon. . . And if not tomorrow, then the day after. . . ."   3. ". . .today you can no longer recognize anything. In place of fortifications there is a city. Maybe — because of those days."

Chapter Twenty-Three

ASPECTS OF THE REFUGEE SITUATION *(page 150)*

1. (d) Directly after the Six Day War in 1967   2. (b) The sober realization that the Palestinians were the crux of the Middle East conflict; and that if their problem were not solved, there could be no negotiated settlement with the various Arab governments   3. Open Bridges   4. False (This policy was in force during and after the Yom Kippur War.)   5. True

HISTORY'S HEADLINES *(page 152)*

1. Promise to Arabs in Israel's Declaration of Independence   2. Influx of Jewish immigrants to Israel, particularly from the Arab countries   3. The problem of the Palestinian refugees   4. The Open Bridges Policy   5. Siah Lohamim

EDITORIALS *(page 153)*

1. The refusal of Arab governments to consider Israeli proposals toward a solution of the refugee problem   2. The issue of allowing anti-Israel propaganda to be incorporated into textbooks used in the refugee camps, supported by the UN   3. The influx of vast numbers of Jewish immigrants to Israel

AN ARAB TOUR OF ISRAEL *(page 156)*

1. Ashkelon   2. Kibbutz Hatzerim   3. Haifa   4. Eilat   5. Tel Aviv (and Jaffa)   6. Beersheba   7. Jerusalem   8. Arad

Chapter Twenty-Four

A SEARCH FOR UNDERSTANDING *(page 160)*

1. National sport;   bulmus   2. Roots;   continuity: Arab   3. Bible; National Bible Quiz (Hidon HaTanach)   4. Kibbutz Galuyot (the Ingathering of the Exiles);   making the Desert Bloom   5. Masada; Dead Sea Scrolls;   synagogue

SPEECHES OF SIGNIFICANCE *(page 161)*

4;   8;   5;   6;   7;   1;   2;   3

TRUE OR FALSE? *(page 164)*

1. True   2. False   3. False   4. True   5. False   6. True   7. False
8. True

AN ARCHAEOLOGICAL BIBLE QUIZ *(page 165)*

1. The Exodus of the children of Israel from Egypt   2. Abraham's fulfillment of God's command (which turned out to be a test of faith) to sacrifice his son, Isaac   3. The Tribes of Israel demanding that the prophet Samuel anoint a king, so that they would be a nation like all other nations   4. Moses' discovery of the Golden Calf, upon his return from Mount Sinai, and his smashing of the sacred tablets   5. A celebration in honor of the birth of Isaac to Abraham, age 100, and Sarah, age 90

Chapter Twenty-Five

FORMS OF GOVERNMENT *(page 168)*

Here are the answers; you explain the reasons.   1. A   2. T   3. T
4. P   5. A   6. T   7. A

WORD SCRAMBLE *(page 170)*

1. three   2. two   3. opinions   4. Jews

Chapter Twenty-Six

A SEARCH FOR UNDERSTANDING *(page 173)*

1. (e) Are experts in Arab customs and culture   2. (d) Enjoys a luxurious life-style   3. (g) The Histadrut   4. (c) Ideologists and revolutionaries
5. (b) Are active in senior citizens groups and golden age societies.

PROBABLY TRUE OR FALSE, AND WHY? *(page 174)*

Here are the true or false answers; you explain why.   1. True   2. True
3. True   4. False   5. True   6. False   7. True   8. False

WHO SAID WHAT TO WHOM? *(page 175)*

Here are the answers; you explain why.   1. V to S   2. O to A   3. V to O   4. A to S   5. S to V   6. S to A

Chapter Twenty-Eight

PROBABLY TRUE OR FALSE, AND WHY? *(page 187)*

1. True   2. False   3. False   4. True   5. True   6. False   7. True

THE LESSONS OF HISTORY *(page 188)*

5;   3;   6;   2;   1;   4

ODD PERSON OUT *(page 192)*

1. (e) A sense of outrage over the evergrowing economic distance between the Israeli haves and have-nots   2. (c) Feel that modern Israel bears no resemblance at all to the original Zionist blueprint   3. (d) Believe that his country's Middle East policy has been consistent since 1948   4. (d) Want to attend an ulpan when he returns home

---

Chapter Twenty-Nine

TRUE OR FALSE? *(page 197)*

1. True   2. False   3. False   4. True   5. True   6. True   7. True
8. False

WORD SCRAMBLE *(page 200)*

1. Insecurity   2. Ambition   3. Ignorance   4. Cowardice   5. Shame
Circled letters: Education